7 - 99.

Readymade Business Speeches

Readymade
Business
Speeches

BARRY TURNER

**KOGAN
PAGE**

First published in Great Britain in 1989 by
Kogan Page Limited, 120 Pentonville Road,
London N1 9JN

British Library Cataloguing in Publication Data

Turner, Barry
  Readymade business speeches
  1. Public speaking. Manuals. For businessmen
  I. Title
  808.5'1

  ISBN 1-85091-638-1
  ISBN 1-85091-639-X Pbk

Printed and bound in Great Britain by
Biddles Ltd, Guildford

Contents

1

Preparing a Speech

One of the classic nightmares has to do with acting, though it is by no means restricted to actors. The victim is standing in the wings, waiting to go on stage to play the role of a life-time. Spot on cue he steps forward to rapturous applause. And in that awful, terrifying moment he knows, he just knows, that he cannot remember a single word of his lines.

The dream can be so powerful as to deter some people from ever getting to their feet in public, let alone participating in amateur dramatics.

But their fears are exaggerated.

While stage fright is real enough it is seldom so devastating as to produce a total memory block. The actor who has to walk off because his mind has gone blank is a rare bird indeed. Having rehearsed his lines and run over them many times in his head, it is actually very difficult for him to lose the lot. He might stumble over a few words, but with a little help from his friends, he can usually find his way back to the script.

The risk of a public speaker drying up is greater. He is on his own, for one thing. There is rarely anyone around—a prompter, other actors—to pull him out of the mess. Any speaker who looks to his chairman for guidance in his hour of need is naively optimistic.

But isolation is not the chief reason why public speakers come unstuck.

We have all encountered the public speaker who trusts to luck. At best he arms himself with a few facts and figures, jots down some notes and thinks up a funny story while driving to the meeting. That should do it, he thinks. After all, he is a busy man.

But then, it only takes an unexpected change of circumstances—an audience of a hundred, say, instead of the anticipated small, friendly gathering—to create terror in the heart, a seizing up of the mental processes and embarrassment all round.

> Ladies and gentlemen—how nice it is to see you all here. I had no idea so many of you would turn up, considering the weather and one thing and another. Yes... Well... I'm certainly glad to see you all here... Er... And I want to say, 'Welcome'... Yes, indeed... and in saying 'Welcome' I feel a bit like Groucho Marx who told his audience, 'Hello, I must be going.' And so... Without more ado I'll hand you on to...

What humiliation! And all the more galling because it was self-inflicted.

Allow time for preparation and rehearsal

A good speech is like a good story. It must have a structure with a beginning, a middle and an end; a logical sequence of thoughts which leads to a satisfying conclusion.

Paradoxically, the preparation of a speech should begin with the conclusion.

Decide on the objective

Even the simplest speech—a vote of thanks, say—has an end in view. The speaker wants the audience to feel pleased with the proceedings and to round off the occasion with hearty applause.

An after-dinner speech may aim to raise money for charity; a speech in support of an election candidate will succeed only if it gains votes; a manager's speech to his workforce usually presumes the need to win co-operation for a change in company policy. And so on.

Having decided on the objective:

Identify the main points to be put across
Suppose there is a protest meeting against a new stretch of motorway planned to skirt the village of Little Wallop. As a leading citizen and a vociferous opponent of the motorway, you are called upon to address the meeting.

The objective is clear — to build up support for the protest movement by winning over the undecided.

To do this, pinpoint the arguments that will make the strongest impact on the audience.

The motorway will cut clear across countryside of great natural beauty; it will destroy the peace of the village by attracting hordes of day trippers and it will depress the value of residential property.

These three arguments go to make the core of the speech.

A structure is beginning to emerge. But it may not be as strong as it looks at first glance.

Anticipate objections
In the case of the Little Wallop motorway, there may be tradespeople in the community who would welcome an influx of visitors as a stimulus to business. How can they be persuaded to change their views? Certainly, their opinions can't be ignored. A speaker who is left floundering in the wake of rational criticism should not expect sympathy from his audience.

Resolve problems
There is an overlap here with the last point, but in this context the problems are those raised by the speaker himself. For example, even if Little Wallop is united in its opposition to the motorway, the campaign will surely fail if there is no suggestion for an alternative route. To be taken seriously, a speaker must work towards a positive conclusion.

At this stage of the preparation, a speech will consist of a pile of notes, possibly, but not necessarily, arranged in some sort of order. The temptation now is to hurry on to the finish. But the practised speaker allows time for reflection. Over a few days, thoughts occur of ways in which the substance of a speech can be strengthened and its presentation sharpened.

Look out for relevant anecdotes

Jokes should be used sparingly (it is amazing that the failure rate of jokes, particularly old jokes, does not act as a more powerful deterrent) but human interest stories always make an impact.

Personal experience—and a long memory—usually serve as the most fruitful source for material. But once we have a clear idea of what we are looking for, relevant bits and pieces of information turn up with encouraging frequency. This is not mere coincidence, of course. It is just that when we think hard about a subject we are bound to notice references to it which might otherwise pass us by.

Make notes along the way. There is nothing quite so infuriating as finding a good story, and then forgetting all about it until after the speech is delivered.

The next stage is critical. Having gathered together material and decided on a rough order of contents, it is time to:

Write out the speech in full

Those who balk at what they regard as unnecessary drudgery should beware that while an individual's ability to write clearly, logically and persuasively is not in itself a guarantee of success as a public speaker, a person who cannot organise his thoughts on paper will almost certainly fail as a speaker.

This will bring immediate objections.

What about actors? Some of the finest actors are hopeless writers. But on stage they are using someone else's words, someone else's character. In performance, actor and writer are as one.

What about the politicians and preachers? There are self-proclaimed orators whose words, on paper, lack force or even sense. But this goes to prove the point. Such people are *not* good speakers. They are strong on delivery, not on content. They may have the power to whip up a crowd into a frenzy—even inspire some extravagant act of dedication or commitment—but the effect is short-lived. When their listeners start thinking rationally about what has been said, the doubts creep in.

This is certainly true of modern business where, in a vigorously competitive environment, defective reasoning is a sure money-loser.

A successful speaker knows precisely what he wants to say *before* he gets to his feet. He has written it all down — and he has tested the logic of his arguments. Then, even if he is not the most compelling performer in the world, he can at least be sure that he will be listened to with respect. And he will always score over the speaker who falls back on the gift of the gab — the last refuge of the bore and the simpleton.

To write a speech is to discover in good time its strengths and weaknesses.

An argument which seemed clear enough when tried out in general conversation may appear far too convoluted on the printed page. A witticism once heard at a party is perhaps not quite so hilarious in a formal context. Previously minor thoughts, on the other hand, can gain stature when seen in relationship to the rest of the speech. They need to be given stronger emphasis.

This is the half-way mark. The speech is written; it is time to go into rehearsal. Before doing so, we can pause for a recap by checking the progress of another speaker who already has a good working knowledge of the rules.

Adam Williams, the managing director of a travel agency, has been invited to speak to a conference of hoteliers. His subject is the British tourist industry and its prospects.

He welcomes the opportunity. As someone who has close contact with overseas visitors, he has a thing or two to say about the standards of hotel service. This is his chance to get across his arguments to the very people who can solve the problems.

Thinking over the possibilities of how he might best approach his subject, Adam comes up with a working title for his speech: 'The Tourist Industry and Its Future. Are We in Danger of Losing Out to Our Competitors?'

A bit pedestrian, perhaps. But the title expresses the objective of the speech — to show that while the tourist industry is booming, future prosperity depends on giving value for money. He can tick off rule one.

Having advanced thus far, there is an awful temptation to assume that the rest is plain sailing. Another speaker might launch off in the traditional way, thanking the chairman for inviting him and declaring what an honour it is to address such an illustrious audience. He would then allow himself a

little joke about a mix-up on bookings which compelled two
honeymoon couples to share a single bedroom before launching into a spirited attack on shoddy standards.

Simple and straightforward. And a near certain flop, as
Adam is aware.

He knows that if his criticisms are to carry weight he must
be specific. Since he will have time to develop only two or
three main points he also needs to be selective. He is on to
the second rule of speech-making, to build up the core of the
speech.

Adam jots down a few ideas:

● Britain has many outstanding tourist attractions
  including a much-loved capital, an admired cultural
  heritage, historical monuments and splendid scenery.
● Tourists praise all this but are less than complimentary
  about hotels and their standards of service.
● The position might not be so serious if high prices
  guaranteed excellent service. In fact, some of the best
  tourist hotels are those which charge modest rates.
● For the moment the tourist industry is booming but
  there could be a rapid turnaround if, for example, there
  was another bad summer or the dollar weakened
  against the pound.

Now Adam is making headway. He has a clear objective in
mind and a fair idea of the message he wants to impart.

But he can be sure that his views will attract strong
counter-arguments.

For example, some hoteliers will argue that the high-
season demand for accommodation is so great as to enable
them to charge whatever they think fit. Why should they
not maximise profits? To reduce prices will merely attract
more low-income tourists. The only sensible policy is to concentrate on the up-market free spenders.

Adam knows that he cannot defeat this argument by
appealing for fair play. In the absence of a convincing rebut-
tal, his audience will choose what seems to them the easiest
route to prosperity. Marshalling his thoughts, he comes up
with a three-part response.

1 Even the big spenders, he will point out, do not like to
  feel they are throwing money away. If word gets around

that leading British hotels are a rip-off, tourists will soon veer away to countries where they are treated with greater respect.

2 A distinction must be made between London and the rest of the country. In London, for the moment anyway, the attractions of the capital outweigh complaints about high prices and inferior services. Elsewhere, tourism is still an infant industry which needs more reasonably priced, quality hotel accommodation to help it grow.

3 It is a big mistake to ignore the interests of the less affluent tourists. They are the future. If the tourist industry is to grow it must cater for a higher proportion of middle-income visitors.

The framework of Adam's speech is beginning to take shape. But it is still lacking a major component. Having raised problems, Adam now has a responsibility to his audience. He must offer practical solutions. It is all very well to criticise, but what can be done to improve matters?

- Hoteliers should take a longer-term view of their interests. By trying harder to satisfy this season's customers they will stimulate business for years to come.
- The hotel chains should think more about investment in areas outside London to help spread the tourist business beyond the capital.
- There should be more co-operation between hotels and local government to ensure good back-up services, such as cheap and convenient parking.
- The standards of training need to be improved at all levels.

It is time for Adam to take stock. He has the substance of a good speech but he is in need of back-up material; a quote, perhaps, from a well known authority to lend weight to his arguments; a few telling statistics; maybe a joke or two to help liven up the proceedings.

In casting about for snippets, Adam reflects that he is still lacking a strong opening for his speech. Some will argue that he should have thought of this before. They are wrong. It is easier to come up with the right words after deciding the contents of the speech. To do otherwise is to risk launching off with remarks which have little to do with the way the main theme is developed. So much time is wasted by speakers who spend hours on a clever introduction, only to abandon it in the very last stage of preparation in favour of a late but more appropriate idea.

The speech must start with a bang, words that will make the audience sit up and take notice.

Adam likes the idea of using a quotation. What was it Robert Louis Stevenson once said? 'To travel hopefully is a better thing than to arrive.' To which, the modern tourist might reply, 'On the money I'm paying out, I want more than that. I want the arrival to live up to my expectations. Why must I always be disappointed?'

But no, it won't work. The link across from Stevenson to the defects of contemporary travel is too laboured.

Another idea occurs when Adam spots a newspaper interview with Michael Montague, former head of the English Tourist Board. But Montague's comments on hotels are fiercely provocative.

'Often supercilious and unwelcoming...restaurants offer menus in French that no one understands...hotel prices are astronomically high for casual visitors with package prices secretly fixed behind the scenes.'

Powerful stuff; and all too likely to offend the audience if it is brought into play too early in the speech.

Adam changes tactics. A more subtle strategy is called for. His criticisms have to be couched in a way that will make them acceptable to the audience. This suggests opening on an optimistic note.

Having made up his mind on that score, he attempts his first draft:

> Ladies and gentlemen.
>
> Every one of us here today has good reason to be proud. We are all part of Britain's fastest growing industry—tourism.
>
> The figures are staggering. Visitors to this country will spend over £7 billion

this year. Add this to the holiday spending of UK residents and the total is close to £18 billion.

The importance of tourism to the national economy can hardly be overestimated. Direct employment by the industry accounts for 900,000 people, some 50 per cent more than agriculture. Of course, hotels are responsible for a big share of this but their indirect impact on employment is perhaps even more significant.

Hotels and restaurants are themselves purchasers of a huge range of products from crockery to carpets and cooking equipment to air conditioning. They account for a large part of the business handled by the car hire firms which, in turn, help employment by buying vehicles manufactured in Britain.

Then there is the impact on the construction industry. Hotels and catering spend up to £100 million a year on new buildings and not much less on equipment. An investment of this order supports some 40,000 jobs.

No wonder the government picks out tourism as one of the best prospects for cutting unemployment. More than most, our industry is labour intensive. Even if some of the work is seasonal and insecure, it is quite a thought that every additional 50 tourists promises the employment of at least one extra person.

That is the good news. For the bad news we need go no further than any one of numerous opinion surveys. The consensus seems to be that tourists like the country and its people, they admire our cultural heritage, they are excited by London and they think our policemen are wonderful—but they most emphatically do not like the prices they have to pay for what they see as inferior standards of service.

Hotels take the brunt of the attack.

What about this for a frank opinion? 'Hotels are often supercilious and unwelcoming... restaurants offer menus in French that no one, least of all the waiters, understands... hotel prices are astronomically high for casual visitors...'

As it happens, this is not the view of a tourist. If it was so, it might easily be dismissed as the over-emotional reaction of a particularly unlucky traveller. But there is more to it than that. Much more. The words were spoken by Michael Montague, the former head of the English Tourist Board. And he should know.

Now, I want to be clear that I am not suggesting that all hotels short-change their customers. On the contrary. There are many good hotels which charge modest prices and set a high standard of service. But they are in the minority. In London particularly, there is an urgent need for improvements.

Some of you, I know, will disagree. Tourism *is* a boom industry, more visitors come here every year—so why should we bother with change? It would be throwing money away.

But I need only remind you that tourism is a very fickle industry. In next to no time, a boom can become a slump. We have only to think of the disastrous consequences for the Italian resorts when they acquired an unsavoury reputation for street crime or for the French Riviera when it was

hit by a succession of forest fires—or
for our own tourist industry when the
Americans bombed Libya.

Just as serious, in my view, is the
threat of a reaction against greedy
and unprincipled hoteliers. Even those
visitors who have plenty to spend
appreciate value for money. If word
gets around that certain British hotels
are a rip-off, they will soon veer away
to countries where they are treated
with greater respect. I know London
will always act as a powerful magnet,
but every other tourist centre is
vulnerable.

There is another vital factor to bear in
mind. If tourism is to continue to
expand, we must make a stronger
appeal to the middle-income range of
visitors—those who are quite prepared
to pay for their enjoyment but do not
have money to throw around. It would
be catastrophic if we priced them out
of the market.

What then can be done to improve the
position?

To those hoteliers who are providing a
decent service at a decent price I say,
put pressure on those who are letting
the side down. Turn the screws—tight.
You will be doing us all a favour.

To the big chains, I say, invest in
development out of London. We
desperately need good hotels north of
Watford.

And improve training for all staff. At
the very least, hotel receptionists and
waiters could do with lessons in
simple friendliness.

To the tourist industry as a whole, I
say, let us try harder to co-operate
with government on the provision of

decent services, such as cheap and
convenient parking in the major cities.

Let us do all this in the sure
knowledge that we have a great
opportunity before us. If we give our
customers value for money, they will
return time and time again and
encourage others to follow their
example. If we treat them badly they
will stay away.

The choice is ours. Surely it is not a
difficult choice to make.

Thank you.

Be spontaneous—but be careful

Bear in mind, this is only the first draft and as such it is
likely to be some way short of the finished product. After
running through it a number of times, Adam will change his
mind on details of content and style. But he has at least
decided on the substance of what he wants to say. The hardest part of the job is done.

There is another, more fundamental, sense in which the
speech as made to an audience differs from the speech as
written down. Putting words to paper, we are naturally and
properly constrained by syntax. We make paragraphs and
sentences with the commas and full stops in the right places.
Ideally, the narrative flow is a strictly logical sequence of
thoughts which should preclude deviation or repetition.

Vocal speech is much less inhibited. This is made evident
by analysing a sample of everyday dialogue. What makes
reasonable sense when heard can take some working out
when reproduced on the page.

Now, look. We've got a right problem
here. If I've said it once, I've said it a
thousand times, we're being asked to
do too much. What? Yes. The Mansell
delivery. It can't be done. Oh I know.
But that was last month. We had a
few slack days. Now it's go go go. I
mean to say. No, not tomorrow either.

> I just can't. All right, you tell me.
> There's not one van in the depot.
> They're all out. So what do I do?

From this we gather there is trouble in the warehouse. We might also conclude that the speaker likes the sound of his own voice. He uses close on a hundred words to convey a message which could be said in a dozen words.

> I do not have a van to spare for the
> Mansell delivery.

Very few people express themselves so succinctly. Because they are interacting with other speakers, thinking and talking at the same time, expressing emotions as well as observations and ideas, the words are bound to come out in a bit of a jumble. Clear and concise thinking is an undoubted virtue but with the best will in the world, conversation must have its murky patches. It is the price we pay for spontaneity.

A good speech is somewhere between a conversation and an article. The speaker cannot digress as the fancy takes him—and 'ums' and 'ahs' and other devices for giving him time to think are definitely out—but he must be able to connect with the audience, emphasising arguments where there are signs of enthusiasm, cutting back on passages which fail to make an impact.

The rehearsal

This brings us to the rehearsal.

It may seem paradoxical to claim that spontaneity can be achieved by running through the same material time and time again, but that is the truth. The more a speech is rehearsed, the more likely it is that the speaker will have the desired sequence of ideas firmly implanted in his mind. He does not have to know every word—indeed it is better if he does not learn the speech like lines in a play—but he must have such a grasp of his subject that he can afford to play with words, to adjust his line of reasoning to suit the mood of the moment, without losing the thread of the main argument.

The alternative, which is to read the speech, is nearly always a disaster. For generations, university dons bored their students rigid with their monotonous recitations. Even today, with our better understanding of the learning process, there are academic lecturers whose lazy habit of reading straight from manuscript guarantees their failure as teachers.

To speak persuasively is to talk directly at the audience, eye to eye, as if in conversation. The type of person who mumbles at the ground is neither liked nor trusted. It is the same with the speaker who buries his head in his notes. After the first few minutes, the disposition of the audience changes from polite interest to indifference to aggravation. He might as well give up and go home.

The first stage of the rehearsal requires the services of a good friend, someone who will sit patiently while the speaker:

Read the speech out loud
The friend must be honest and candid. Does the speech make sense to him? If not, it's back to the drawing board. But that is the worst that can happen. More probably, the friendly critic will suggest that some parts of the speech need elucidation. What seems perfectly clear to the originator of an idea may not be self-evident to the uninitiated.

Never brush aside an appeal for clarification. If one person does not understand, you can be sure that others will share his puzzlement.

Read the speech again
But, this time, without an audience. Concentrate on the sections which, for one reason or another, might present difficulties. What about awkward pronunciations? Long words should be avoided as a matter of course—they nearly always sound pompous and out of place—but even quite ordinary words are apt to writhe out of control. Everybody has his own particular embarrassment. Mine is the word 'ignominy'. I can't even spell it (as testified by the scratchings out on my notes for this book) let alone pronounce it.

Alliteration is always dangerous. Heed the fate of Canon Archibald Spooner whose name is for ever associated with accidental but forgivable slips of the tongue. 'Kinquering Kongs their titles take', is an entirely understandable misreading of the opening lines of a popular hymn and who can blame the poor man for his confused dismissal (in America one might say 'discombobulated dismissal'—but not twice) of an errant student.

'You have deliberately tasted two worms and you can leave Oxford by the next town drain.'

Phraseology which looks harmless on paper can hide within it the threat of a horrible tongue-twister. I once heard a senior manager proclaim the imminent arrival of cashless shopping. Or rather, that is what he tried to do. But 'cashless' juxtaposed with 'shopping' was too much for his larynx. After a couple of tries he told his audience, 'Oh, to hell with it. Maybe it's not so close, after all.'

The terrors of pronunciation can be easily forestalled by a little practice. If speaking a word proves difficult, choose another way of expressing yourself. The English language is not short on synonyms.

Watch out for possible misinterpretation. Words can have different meanings for different people, as anyone who crosses the Atlantic can testify. In the same way, words can change meaning as they traverse age or class barriers.

On the second or third reading of the speech:

Check the timing
Whatever the figure, it will almost certainly be an underestimate. The difference in timing between reading aloud from a script and speaking from memory or from notes can be up to one-third. This is because we tend not to take account of extra words and phrases that creep into a speech once we are released from the set script. So it is that if the speech has a twenty-minute limit and the reading takes half an hour, the contents need to be cut by at least half to avoid running over time.

The penultimate stage of rehearsal is to:

Reduce the speech to key headings and brief notes
Many speakers use a series of cards which, on the day, can serve as crib notes. If this idea appeals, be sure to choose proper cards. Flimsy slips of paper are difficult to hold and easily get muddled. Write or, better still, print in letters that are large enough to see at a glance.

A speaker who uses a form of shorthand should feel confident that he can understand his own abbreviations. Standard acronyms like MD for managing director are no trouble but initials of people, particularly of those who are sharing the platform, can cause problems. Indeed, names should always be spelt out in full. Take to heart the horror story of the first-time chairman who launched into a rousing introduction of a well known personality, proclaiming 'your friend and mine, whose name is known to us all...Mr...er...Mr...er...'

Mr er was not best pleased.

Rehearse the speech from the notes

This is where the speaker gets into his stride. Remember, this is not simply a memory exercise. The sequence of thoughts must be right but thereafter this final stage of rehearsal should concentrate on the flow of language. The words may be different at each try: that does not matter in the least. The important thing is to feel comfortable with the central arguments. Do they hang together and make sense? If a speaker cannot convince himself he will certainly not convince anybody else.

With confidence comes expression, the deployment of personality to lift the speech from the level of automatic delivery to the heights of a true performance.

Expression has much to do with sense of timing, knowing how to reinforce the impact of words by varying the pace and level of enunciation.

In the days of mass meetings, when political speakers could face audiences of up to 30,000, the leading exponents of the art were masters of timing. You have only to think of Churchill's ability to inspire his listeners.

There is the example of the famous joke—not a joke in the true sense at all—created by Churchill's delivery.

'When I warned the French that Britain would fight on alone whatever they did, their generals told their prime minister and his divided cabinet, "In three weeks England will have her neck wrung like a chicken." (Pause) 'Some chicken;' (long pause for

a ripple of laugher) 'some neck.' (A
huge roar of laughter and tumultuous
applause.)

It is quite easy to imagine that another, less gifted, speaker
would have thrown away that last line, not even guessing at
its potential as a rallying call to an entire nation.

Of course, with Churchill, the deep growl of his voice was
itself an inspiration, evoking the image of the bulldog breed,
indefatigable and invincible. If his speeches had been delivered in the light whispery tones of, say, Neville Chamberlain,
they could not have succeeded.

The voice is an integral part of a speaker's personality and
can work for or against him according to circumstances.

Short of elocution lessons there is not too much we can do
about our voices except to judge the tone that is best suited
to a particular audience and try to adapt accordingly.

Talking into a tape recorder and listening critically to the
playback can help. Many who do this are surprised at the
sound of their own voices. 'Do I really sound like that?' It
may be too late to change a pronounced accent (anyway,
accents are seldom a problem until they overwhelm language) but it is possible to correct a fault like talking too
quickly or too slowly.

Personality has as much to do with appearance as with
sound. A speaker must look and act the part. Dress sense is
an advantage (nothing too startling or the costume will compete for attention), but more important is the way a speaker
actually presents himself to an audience. What do they see,
up there on the platform? A common sight is the tailor's
dummy, fastened by the hands to a table or lectern, appar-
ently incapable of moving a muscle. At the other extreme is
the wild flailer, arms and legs working away as if on an exercise machine.

Somewhere between the two is the speaker who feels at
home in his own body. He uses arm movements to suggest a
wide embrace ('we are all in this together'), he clenches a fist
to show determination or points skywards to indicate outside forces ('the government will not get away with this') but
he takes care not to point directly at the audience who will
interpret the gesture as an accusation.

This speaker knows when to put on a serious look and when to smile. Above all, he knows when to smile.

We left Adam Williams pondering the draft of his speech on the future of the tourist industry. It is not quite right, as he is the first to admit, but it is a fair start.

Casting about for an honest critic he can think of no one better than Mark, his teenage son, a first-year college student who fancies himself as an impartial observer of the social scene. Like all children of a certain age, Mark is in no way inhibited from giving his father a forthright opinion.

After hearing the speech, Mark comes up with some pertinent views.

'There are too many statistics in the first two minutes', he tells Adam. 'People can't take all those figures at one go. Another thing: the speech is altogether too heavy. Can't we have a bit of light relief?'

Adam takes his son's comments to heart. On rereading the speech he finds that the opening passages do sound ponderous. But he does not want to discard what he sees as highly relevant facts. His remedy is to transfer some figures from the speech to a flip chart which will stand beside him on the platform.

As for the light relief, Adam knows he will have problems in holding his audience to a mood of deadly seriousness. But he is not keen on slipping in jokes for their own sake. Experience has shown that he does not take easily to the role of funny man. On the other hand, he has a ready supply of weird, wonderful and true stories of tourists' tribulations in a foreign land. Only recently he had been told about the Japanese visitor who, asking to try British wine, was sold a bottle of whisky.

After some rewriting and another read through (this time with an eye on the clock), Adam reduces his speech to a series of short headings. This is how it looks:

● Intro. Tourism fastest growing industry.
● Importance to national economy.
● Central role of hotels.
● But—much criticism of inferior services.
● Michael Montague's quote.

- Funny/peculiar stories of bad treatment of tourists.
- Why we must improve services.
- Risk of slump.
- Importance of middle-income tourists.
- What can be done to improve services?
    Good hotels to lead campaign for change.
    More hotels needed out of London.
    Better training.
    Co-operate with government.
- Choice is ours.

Now Adam tries the speech for memory. On the first two or three attempts he loses his way or forgets an important section. But with practice comes confidence and before long he is on such familiar terms with his material he can experiment with different ways of saying the same thing. By this process he discovers that the ending works better if he gives it more punch, allowing suitable pauses for his words to sink in.

> Tourism is big business. (Pause) But it still has a long way to go. The question is, are we going to sit back and enjoy the success we have or (voice rising) press on to greater things? (Pause) The time to make that choice (with great emphasis) is now. (Pause—and then quietly) Tomorrow may be too late.
>
> Thank you.

There are still several days to go before Adam will stand before his audience. He has done all he can by way of preparation. Or has he? The speech is ready, it is true. But as a cautious man, Adam will not feel entirely happy until he has checked out the venue. He wants to be sure that what he says is heard and understood.

Come the day

It may not be possible to find out much about the place where the speech is to be given or even to meet the organisers of the programme before the actual day. If this is the case:

Arrive early

Get the feel of the conference room. Is there anything that gives you cause to worry? For example, when you stand on the platform, can you be seen clearly by everybody in the audience? For the listener it is infuriating not to be able to observe without engaging in physical contortion. Is there a table or lectern? Many speakers like to have somewhere to put their notes and other references they might need.

But bear in mind that a large and ungainly piece of furniture can easily become a barrier between speaker and audience. So often the lectern turns out to be a false friend. It is either too low, which means that the speaker has to bend forward as if making ready to sprint into the audience, or so high that it masks his performance. I once heard an entire address delivered through a lavish bouquet of flowers placed strategically in front of the lectern. Unwilling to abandon his prop, the speaker tried to peer round the foliage; when that became too much of a strain, he simply retreated behind it. I can remember the flowers quite clearly but not a single word of the speech.

What about acoustics?

Check the equipment

There is a tendency nowadays for conference organisers to provide microphones, however small the meeting room. For anything up to 2,000 square feet, a mike should not be needed. Even in a much larger room, unless it has a design peculiarity like a very high ceiling, a mike can be more trouble than it is worth.

The fact is, most speakers are not used to hearing their voices amplified. Having rehearsed without the support of audio equipment, it is not easy to adapt quickly to the demands of sophisticated technology. There is a tendency to be either overawed by the microphone and to speak too softly or, remaining blissfully unaware of its power, to bellow at the audience like a revivalist preacher.

When a microphone is provided it is wise to try it out. If it seems unnecessary or if there is any hint that it might be unreliable, simply ask for it to be switched off for your part of the proceedings.

Rehearse the use of visual aids
Even a flip chart can prove hazardous. Felt pens have a nasty habit of running dry at a critical moment (make sure there are plenty of spares) and pages stick together.

As for overhead and slide projectors, videos and the mounting profusion of yet more ambitious devices for holding audience attention, sod's law dictates that whatever can go wrong, eventually will go wrong—at the worst possible moment.

To minimise the risk, test and retest all equipment (ideally there should be a qualified technician on hand) and check there is a generous reserve of bulbs, plugs and batteries.

Brief the chairman
It is in the nature of chairmen not to think too clearly about their responsibilities until the last moment. Despite a wealth of evidence to the contrary, they assume that throwing together a few introductory remarks is just a matter of re-arranging a few well known words and phrases.

> Delighted to see you all here... very important occasion... panel of eminent speakers... quite sure we will all benefit from their wisdom... don't want to take up valuable time... our first speaker is...

To adopt this tedious formula is unfair on the opening speaker who has the job of rousing the audience from the lethargy inflicted on them by the chairman. But this is not the worst that can happen.

A chairman can mispronounce or forget names, muddle the sequence of events, say too much or too little about each speaker or, most frequently, set the wrong tone with an ill-timed announcement on matters entirely unconnected with the business in hand.

The classic instance of this last failing is the chairman who, before calling on the first speaker, declared that he had some sad news to impart. Poor old Tom Walker who had been with the company for 40 years and had only retired last Thursday had died peacefully in his sleep. 'Let us all stand in silence', he boomed, 'to mourn the passing of a fine man.' After the customary two minutes the audience resumed their seats, the chairman returned to his script and the first speaker tore up all his jokes.

There is no guarantee against a bad chairman but a speaker can minimise the risk by writing his own introduction. This way he will stem the flow of superlatives ('this extraordinary man...one of the finest brains in the business...great sense of humour...') which can be difficult to justify in a 30-or 40-minute address. Also, he can hope to deter the chairman from occupying too much time.

But handing over a potted life history has its dangers. A lesson to us all is the terrible experience of an after-dinner speaker who, trying to be helpful, sent the chairman a two-page account of his career, as prepared by a lecture agency. On the night, the grateful recipient excelled himself with a precise rendition of every word in the guest's CV including his address, telephone number and his scale of fees for private functions.

As the moment approaches:

Make a last-minute check that all is in place
Not least the clothes you stand up in. This may seem unnecessarily fastidious but a curiosity of dress, such as a strategic zip left undone, can be a compulsive distraction.

Just before speaking, take a deep breath
It helps to settle the butterflies. But accept that nervousness is part of the game. Conscientious rehearsal minimises the risk of drying up but there is always the possibility of losing the thread of an argument or missing out some vital fact. (If this happens, remember that an audience will sympathise with a speaker who makes honest mistakes—and recovers.) There is no shame in pausing to admit the fault and to check notes before resuming. There is no virtue in floundering about hoping that no one will notice the mistake. They always do.

Adapt the tone of the speech to the surroundings
If the audience turns out to be much smaller than expected (say a flu epidemic reduces the ranks) it may be necessary to abandon the impassioned call to action in favour of a gentler, more informal appeal. But whatever the technique, the

speaker must communicate enthusiasm and conviction. To sound half-hearted is to invite listeners to respond in like manner.

Be grateful for unexpected laughs
Some speakers are thrown by the reaction to an unintentional joke. But audience laughter, even when it is at the expense of the speaker (when he unknowingly commits a dreadful pun, for example) is always friendly. Take it as a sign of support.

Associate with the audience
Look to the front and look at the audience, not at the tops of their heads or at their knees.

Refer more to 'us' (joined in common cause) than to 'you' (by implication, the miserable lot out there) and 'me' (the one who knows it all).

Stick to the allotted time
It is so easy to overrun when the mood of the audience is swinging in your favour. Why not hold them for just a little longer with another compelling observation or a rousing argument?

Resist! Overrunning is the deadly sin of public speaking. Many a good speech has ended badly because the speaker did not know when to stop.

Save questions to the end
Even friendly questions can disrupt the flow of argument if they are taken in the middle of a speech. Hostile questions can be devastating. Think of the shambles of House of Commons oratory when it is interrupted by points of order or information.

If the speech is at all contentious it is bound to spark off discussion. Adam Williams, for example, knows that his audience of hoteliers will contain several unrepentant critics of his thesis eager to take him to task. But he must resist the urge to engage in a full-scale row. A speaker who loses his temper invites yet more barks from his opponents. Meanwhile, those who came to listen find their interest wandering from the content of the speech to the thrill of a slanging match.

To keep a question and answer session on an even keel, the speaker should try to disarm his opponents before they get too dangerous.

> Mr Williams, you seem to be suggesting that all the problems of the tourist industry can be dumped on the forecourts of the big hotels. You haven't said very much about travel agents and some of the dodgy tricks they get up to. Shouldn't you put your own house in order before coming here to criticise us?

It must be tempting for Adam to snap back.

> It is easy enough to avoid your own problems by pointing the finger at someone else. Your tone of voice suggests I have hit a raw nerve. OK, so there may be some travel agents who are less than efficient but they have nothing to do with the points at issue which are the standards and charges set by the hotels. Are you claiming that the hotels are giving the best possible service?

Back comes the questioner, his temper fraying fast.

> I'm not saying anything about hotels. All I'm saying is that you pick your arguments to suit a one-sided case...

And so on, and so on until sections of the audience start drifting away.

Adam Williams will do better to go for a more judicious response.

> I understand how you feel. I do not want to give the impression that hotels are to blame for all our ills. Of course that is not the case. But I think we should concentrate on one thing at a time. I am happy to return to talk about travel agents and their failings.

> But, for now, do you have a specific
> question on the subject in hand?

It is almost impossible now for the questioner to stick to his first line of attack. If he does so, the audience will think him a bore and will support an appropriate reprimand from the speaker or his chairman.

Another way of neutralising hostility is to ask, very politely for the question to be repeated.

> I don't think I quite understand your
> point. Would you mind telling me
> again?

But the questioner has exhausted his passion. When he gets to his feet again it is to deliver a much-diluted attack which, in turn, invites a calm, reasoned reply.

It remains only for the chairman to propose a vote of thanks and for the audience to raise the roof with their applause.

Postscript: Adam Williams did rather well with his speech to the hoteliers. They even laughed at his jokes. Now he gets other invitations to appear on the conference circuit. It takes up a lot of time but he knows that his reputation as a speaker has added to his authority as a businessman. And he has the income to prove it.

2

The Company Presentation

A presentation is selling by another name. All the skills that a salesman brings to bear on an individual customer should be as much in evidence when a senior executive is putting the case for his firm to be awarded a major contract.

The most common form of company presentation is a small and deceptively cosy affair. The decision-makers—seldom more than a dozen of them and possibly as few as two or three—gather round a conference table while the speaker does his best to persuade them that he has the answer to their problems.

The wise presenter resists the apparent informality of the proceedings. He gives as much preparation and planning to his task as he would to a conference speech for a thousand delegates.

Making the best of it

Choose your moment

Timing is a critical factor, not only the length of the presentation and its pace of delivery, but the hour of day for which it is scheduled. Presentations tend to come in groups, with a succession of rivals parading one after the other.

As a general rule, a slot before lunch is more likely to produce a good result than one after lunch. This is not to suggest that business people are excessive eaters and drinkers—many are notoriously spartan in their culinary habits. But it takes only one over-indulger to disrupt an afternoon presentation. His evident lack of interest can easily spread to his companions who, in the nature of things, will be feeling the strain of attending to a succession of speakers all dealing with the same subject.

A really good speaker can enliven the meeting with the delivery of a startlingly novel idea—that the job under consideration can be carried out at half the anticipated price, for example. But few presentations allow for such dramatic interventions. To overcome the resistance of a dozy audience, most speakers resort to talking louder or faster—or trying to do both simultaneously. In any event, the chances of saving the day are slim indeed.

The odds on a presentation leading to a contract shorten considerably when the speaker can make a morning pitch, preferably just before lunch or a coffee break because then he will be a natural choice for social conversation.

> What did you think of the last one?
>
> Alan Williams? Not bad; not bad at all. About as good as that chap we heard at the beginning. What was his name?

You see, he has forgotten already.

Trying for best position in the day's programme may call for subterfuge. The prospective client will try to sidetrack any discussion on the order of appearance by arbitrarily declaring the agenda well in advance.

> Dear Mr Williams,
>
> We are delighted that you will be able to join us on June 14th.
>
> Your presentation is scheduled for 2.00 p.m. but, of course, if you would like to arrive earlier, you will be very welcome.
>
> Yours etc.

There follows a telephone call from Alan Williams.

> I'm very much looking forward to the 14th. There's just one thing. Is there any chance of switching my presentation to the morning session? I want to

try to get back to my office by mid-
afternoon which really means setting
off at one at the latest.

An appeal from one businessman to another to co-operate in
saving time is certain of a sympathetic response.

Know your place
Having settled on when the presentation is to be made, the
next priority is to check out the venue. This is important for
any speech but with a presentation there is more chance of
the unwary being taken by surprise. Knowing that he is to
face a six-member committee, a presenter can take it badly
when he is ushered into a meeting room big enough to
accommodate the London Symphony Orchestra. Equally, it
can be thoroughly off-putting if he is expected to set up complex visual aids in a corner of the managing director's office.

The adage about the forewarned being forearmed comes
to mind. But even when the venue is known, there remains
the problem of setting up the presentation to achieve the
best possible impression.

Visual aids
More than any other area of public speaking, the success or
failure of a presentation can hinge on the imaginative use of
visual aids.

At the very least there should be a flip chart close to hand,
but overhead and slide and video projectors may well be
called into play, not to mention specially constructed mod-
els and charts.

On the well-established principle that a single picture is
worth a thousand words, there is a mighty temptation to
rely too heavily on whizz-bang technology. Revert to the
objective of the presentation—to sell a product or service.
Remember that people buy from people, not from machines.
A speaker will never assert his credibility if he allows his
visual aids to do his work for him.

Another point to keep in mind is that visual aids are not in
themselves interesting. A dull message cannot be trans-
formed by flashing it up on a screen. It will remain a dull
message. For all their self-proclaimed talent for popular

communication, advertising agencies invariably fail to acknowledge this basic truth.

From real life comes the example of an agency presentation in which every word spoken was reproduced in visual form — from 'Hello and Welcome' to 'The End'.

Who are you addressing?

In addition to checking out the venue and the time of the presentation, it is handy to know who precisely will be attending. Being able to identify all the decision-makers by name and by job-title enables the speaker to tailor his presentation to suit the dominant interests of the group.

The central message he wants to put across may remain constant whatever the circumstances, but the way in which it is delivered can vary enormously depending on whether, say, the finance director or a personnel director is chairing the meeting.

Do's and don'ts

Of the familiar rules of speech preparation, there are those which require special emphasis for the writing of a presentation.

Don't be dull

Avoid a dull recitation of facts and figures. It is accepted that the speaker is not on show to entertain his prospective clients. At the same time, a dry-as-dust presentation will almost certainly fail to win votes.

To adapt a lesson from standard training for salesmen, imagine trying to excite an audience into buying an ordinary household object, such as a plain glass vase.

The newcomer to selling might comment on the elegant shape of the vase and its clean-cut lines but very soon he runs out of things to say. And who can blame him? After all, a vase is a vase is a vase. It takes a practised salesman, one who knows the importance of highlighting the features, to show what can be done.

He starts, not with the vase itself but with the purpose to which the vase will be put. He talks about flower arranging, a hobby which attracts hundreds of thousands of devotees.

More adult education and evening classes are devoted to flower arranging than to any other subject. He goes on to explain that the vase we see before us is designed in such a way as to make it ideal for long-stemmed flowers with plenty of bloom. Such is the enthusiasm we have no trouble in visualising a fabulous display of irises or lilies.

The vase is no longer a simple container. By association with a splendid ideal it has taken on an aura of rare taste and sophistication. Any one of us would be proud to own it.

The principle of selling the features applies to any product or service. Except to the specialist there is nothing inherently interesting in a piece of office equipment such as a word processor or a photocopier. It is what they can do that really matters; the time they can save on routine tasks, so that staff can get on with more rewarding work. The detailed mechanics of a new pension scheme can send all but the accountants into a deep sleep. But interest quickly revives when the discussion gets round to the attractions of a comfortable and financially secure retirement.

Don't deviate
Don't waste time trying to prove how clever you are. Faced with a line-up of hard-faced cynics whose collective expression reads 'Impress me!', the speaker may feel compelled to justify himself and his company.

> Cuisine Catering was founded in 1958 by Shaun Andrews. He started in a small way by setting up an assembly plant in a converted garage. Here are some slides of those early days. Little did we know then of the challenges ahead...

All fascinating economic history but totally irrelevant to the matter in hand.

It is not unknown for a presentation to be so extended by self-advertisement that the speaker has to be cut off in mid-flow having failed to deliver a single positive idea.

Don't be pedantic
Don't waste time telling the audience what it already knows.

A presentation may come at the end of a long process of negotiation in which aspects of the proposal, such as the overall budget, have already been settled. It is a common mistake to assume that all previous discussions must be summarised by way of a lead-in to the presentation. But this is to start off on the wrong foot.

> Gentlemen,
>
> I would like to begin with a recap of the conclusions reached in our earlier discussion.

Why? Are the listeners such dimwits that they cannot recall their own formulation of policy? If yes, they should be in different jobs; if no, the feeling they have heard it all before could weaken the impact of any original ideas which happen to crop up later in the presentation.

Similarly, it is not necessary to labour the objective of the exercise. This should be stated clearly and simply in a single sentence. If, say, a new hotel is to be built in the centre of Manchester, the company hoping to provide catering equipment has the objective of installing facilities capable of feeding a specific number of guests and staff. That's it! Yet, typically, whoever is speaking on behalf of Cuisine Catering will be unable to resist the urge to fill out the objective with all manner of extraneous information.

> A new hotel for central Manchester is a long-felt want. A thriving metropolis with a population close on three million, Manchester is a natural focal point for business and for business travellers.

Yes, yes. We know all that. Get on with it.

> In considering the requirements for the hotel, Cuisine has taken into account the anticipated average level of occupancy together with the various demands on the catering facilities ranging from quick snacks to top-level business entertainment.

More platitudes. At some point in the proceedings, it may

well be necessary to discuss the average level of occupancy and the variety of catering expected by the business traveller. But to join all this into a statement of the objective is merely to create a jumble of words and sound without substance.

If the objective needs to be stated at all, it should be as a ringing declaration of intent.

> In satisfying the needs of this great hotel, it is our intention to create one of the most advanced catering facilities in the country.

Allow for feedback

Leave plenty of time for questions. A presentation is not complete without an interrogation.

When listeners remain passive, unable to think of any comments or queries, a speaker can reasonably assume that he has failed to generate interest. Conversely, the speaker who comes away from a presentation feeling like a victim of the Inquisition, may well emerge as the victor.

Think of it this way. If the decision-makers are half-way persuaded that they are on to a winner, they will want to test that impression with an immediate follow-up:

> I can see the need for the restaurants to have an international appeal, but I am still not clear how you would turn out such an extraordinary variety of dishes from the same kitchen.

This is not the sort of question that can be brushed aside with a glib one-liner. It demands a considered and, possibly, quite detailed response. And there may be other equally ticklish questions to follow.

Case study: Selling an idea

Having covered the founding principles of a successful presentation, we can take a closer look at how they work in practice. This calls for a change of scene: from hotel kitchens to the lobby of an old established city bank.

Total Concept is one of several design consultants invited

to submit proposals for the refurbishing of the customer-service area of the headquarters branch of Ashley's Bank. Leading the Total Concept team is Clive Drummond, a recently appointed director who, hitherto, has attended presentations only in a supporting role.

The logistics of the presentation are quite straightforward. Clive is given a mid-morning slot on a date far enough ahead to allow for adequate preparation. The problems lie more in trying to discover what Ashley's hope to achieve. Preliminary meetings with the bank's directors suggest a division between those who want to play safe by sticking to the wing-collar image of prudence and dependability and those who would break with tradition as part of a campaign to attract more of the young, first-time bank customers.

Since neither side yet has the upper hand, it is clear to Clive Drummond that his best chance of success is to come up with a design which will reconcile the conflicting interests.

A close inspection of the banking customer-service area reveals how this might be achieved. The existing layout—a discoloured tiled floor, dark-oak wall panelling, heavy-steel counter grilles—is distinctly uninviting. The gloomy atmosphere is accentuated by a low ornate ceiling supported by four marble pillars. At first glance, nothing short of wholesale demolition is needed to create a lighter, more welcoming environment.

But Clive discovers that the four pillars extend up into a floor of offices immediately above the lobby. How would it be, he wonders, if the height of the lobby was doubled by knocking away the first floor and relocating the office on a four-sided gallery? This would immediately create space and light without destroying the essential character of the building.

It is just a start—but enough to spark off other ideas of how Ashley's might transmute into a bank for the 1990s.

While a series of drawings is prepared, Clive drafts his presentation.

- **Introduction**: the thinking behind the Total Concept design—the need to reconcile homely tradition with modern enterprise.
- **Core proposal**: slide illustrations of the redesign of the customer-service area.

- **Examples** of similar exercises for other clients.
- **Budget.**
- **Timetable.**
- **Questions.**

On the day, Clive arrives at Ashley's head office one hour ahead of time. There is always a chance that a rival company has dropped out at the last moment, leaving a gap in the programme. Whoever is available to step in can earn critical plus-points.

There is another good reason for being early. Clive wants to insure against any last-minute hitches, like a sudden change of venue. If they are not meeting as intended in the board room, Clive needs to find out what alternative is on offer. A room that is much larger than suggested might require a bigger screen for slide projection.

As it turns out, the only problem is the usual one of over-running. Clive is warned that he will be called up to half an hour later than he expected. Sensibly, he has already allowed for this probability by marking off the entire morning for the Ashley presentation.

He uses the spare time to brush up on his presentation, thinking particularly of how to make best use of his visual aids.

In a smallish room there should not be any problems with sight lines. But without a platform Clive needs to make sure that the flip chart and slide screen are high enough to be seen without his listeners having to shuffle their chairs.

He does not have any prepared material for the flip chart but he is sure to want to write up a few figures and key words. The secret, he knows, is always to write large enough for everyone to see clearly, to use different colours for emphasis and never to block the view by standing in front of the flip chart.

It is time. The chairman emerges from the board room to welcome Clive and to show him to his place. He invites Clive to sit while giving his presentation—after all, this is a friendly, informal affair—but the offer is politely rejected. Only when standing can a speaker project the proper degree of enthusiasm. After a few words of introduction, Clive has the floor.

Ladies and gentlemen.

Good morning.

On behalf of Total Concept, thank you for the opportunity to present our ideas for this challenging project.

It is often said that we should not judge by appearances. The advice is sound. Appearances can be deceptive.

For example, a brand-new office block, all steel frame and tinted glass, is not necessarily the breeding ground for innovation and enterprise. To look modern is not the same as being modern.

By the same token, just because the architecture and decor of this building reveal its early Victorian origins, it does not mean that Ashley's Bank has not advanced since the days of its foundation.

But, sadly perhaps, consumer choice does not always depend on thoughtful and logical decisions. The fact is that in our everyday living, most of us *do* rely on appearances. There is not enough time in the day to do anything else.

At this point, a fly-on-the-wall observer would say that Clive had made a good start. Knowing he is up against two opposing factions, he has restricted himself to opening observations which are calculated to meet with common agreement. At the same time, he has started them thinking. Is there a compromise solution?

When we asked a cross-section of customers what they thought of Ashley's Bank, words like 'dependable', 'safe', 'durable' cropped up most frequently.

This is hardly surprising, given Ashley's long-established reputation for secure and steady growth.

The disturbing aspect of this admittedly limited survey is that so few customers seem to realise the enormous changes in Ashley's over the last few years. Notably, the latest advances in computerisation have failed to make the impact that might have been expected. Only one out of eight of those questioned realised that computers play a big part in Ashley's affairs.

I suggest that there is a risk here that what at the moment is seen as an appealing characteristic of Ashley's—that it is a bank which stresses traditional values—could become a liability once the suspicion takes hold that efficiency is losing out to convention.

In submitting our proposals for redesigning the customer-service area of Ashley's head office, we at Total Concept have kept in mind the need to achieve a balanced progression. The great strengths of Ashley's must be seen not as a deterrent but as a stimulant to expansion.

We are approaching the critical stage of the presentation. Clive has said enough to indicate that he understands the problems the Ashley directors are looking to solve. Now he has to come up with some answers.

These pictures will give you an idea of what we have in mind. The first slide shows the customer-service area as we know it.

Now, here is what it would look like if we raised the ceiling to take in the first floor. The marble pillars remain, giving a sense of strength and stature to the lobby.

Also, by pushing back the rear wall and by removing the counter and

> grilles, so, we can open up the whole
> area to allow for a much wider spread
> of business activity with assistants
> having their own work units.

Other slides show the effect of clearing the oak panelling to make it less austere, of introducing some greenery and colourful pictures and of creating a waiting area with comfortable seats and a table for newspapers and promotional material. It is quite a show, with more to come.

> I must emphasise that these ideas are
> not mere speculation. We know they
> can work. As evidence I would like to
> show you just a few examples of our
> work for other clients.

The impression comes across to Clive that his listeners are impressed. He has been watching out for signs of irritation or disagreement—the shuffling of chairs, tapping fingers, loud sighs, grim expressions—but he has spotted nothing untoward.

He feels confident enough to talk about figures.

> I have prepared a detailed budget
> which I will leave with you at the end
> of the presentation. But meanwhile I
> would like to emphasise some features,
> particularly in areas where I believe
> we can make substantial savings.

A clever touch. Clive turns to his flip chart, confident that he has the full attention of his audience. If they had the complete budget in front of them, they would be examining the small print and listening to Clive with only half an ear.

Having disposed of the figures, or at least those figures which give more weight to his argument, Clive builds up to his conclusion with a few words on the timetable.

> We have allowed just one year to
> complete this job. I am sure you will
> agree this is an ambitious target. But
> I know it can be achieved.

> Ladies and gentlemen, I wish to make
> it absolutely clear that Total Concept

> will devote all its skills and energy to the success of this project. We believe we can do a first class job—combining the best in design with the best in banking.
>
> Thank you.

Only now does Clive hand round Total Concept folders containing illustrations seen earlier on screen, the budget and other documents. The speaker who follows the more common practice, of distributing reading material at the beginning of his presentation, has only himself to blame when the attention of his audience wanders.

While the Ashley directors flick through the papers, the chairman asks for the first question. It is not long in coming.

> Would Mr Drummond explain what happens to people currently occupying offices on the first floor? Since we are short of space, I assume that they will need to be relocated in another building.

Clive is ready for this one. Reference to the folder of papers supplements his answer to what is really quite a complex question.

> If you look at drawings 7 and 8, you will see that the new offices positioned along the gallery will provide just as much desk room as there is at the moment. This is because the existing offices have developed in a haphazard way with a consequent unproductive use of space.

There follows a succession of questions on detailed aspects of the design and on costs, questions which suggest to Clive that the meeting is broadly in favour of his proposals. Even so, some directors remain a little uncertain as to Total Concept's ability to handle such an ambitious project.

This worry surfaces in the final question, put by the chairman.

> I think it is fair to say we are all
> impressed with the ideas you have put
> forward, Mr Drummond. But, speaking
> for myself, I do wonder if your
> company is not attempting too much.
> Allowing for the constraints on costs
> and time, are you confident that you
> can meet the targets you have set
> yourself?

There is no going back. Clive has only one possible answer
and he delivers it with all the force at his command.

> I have absolutely no doubt we can
> fulfil our obligations. I need add only
> that I strongly believe our proposal is
> right for Ashley's. I hope you will
> agree.

The inevitable nail-biting wait for the verdict ends after a
few days. Total Concept has won the day. But there is a
catch. The contract has a severe penalty clause which holds
Total Concept to Clive's promise to complete within budget
and within a year. His fellow directors are none too happy at
this. Maybe Clive has let his enthusiasm run away with him.
Only time will tell. They must wait to find out if Clive neg-
lected the last rule of successful presentation.

Never promise what cannot be achieved.

3

Telling Them What They Don't Want to Hear

When there is bad news to impart the compulsion is to get it over with as quickly as possible.

> Ah, Higgins. Come in, won't you? Do sit down. Now, as I'm sure you know, Higgins, times are hard. Very hard indeed. To keep the business afloat, there must be change. Change at the top, change at the middle and change on the shop floor. We must take a lead, Higgins, you can see that, can't you? So it is my painful duty to tell you, your time with this company is over. What? Yes, I know, 35 years is a long time. And don't think I fail to appreciate your loyal service. But there we are. Can't stand in the way of progress, can we? Now I'm sure you have lots of questions so why don't you have a chat with personnel on your way out?

As anyone who has had to take redundancy on the chin will confirm, these nightmare interviews, a throwback to an age of commercial barbarism, do still occur. Paradoxically, it is often the manager with the sharpest sensitivities who commits the worst gaffes. Knowing the dreadful force of the shock he is about to deliver, he gets hopelessly embarrassed and confused. He means well but ends up saying things he will regret for months to come.

It does not have to be this way.

46

The guiding principle for revealing bad news is to try for a counterbalance.

> I realise that early retirement takes a bit of getting used to, Mr Higgins, but remember you will be getting a full pension. Didn't you say you wanted to spend some time with your son in America? Well, now's your chance.

Mr Higgins may still not be the happiest man in the world but at least he goes away with something positive to think about.

The counterbalance rule has its severe limits, of course. Carried too far, it can turn into black farce as in the sick joke about a famous night in American theatre. 'But apart from that, Mrs Lincoln, did you enjoy the play?'

In business, however, where bad news is seldom tragic news, justifying total despair, counterbalancing can do much to ease the pain—and not just in a private interview.

When it comes to making a speech which the audience is not keen to hear, it is well to keep in mind the adage, 'When one door closes, fortune will usually open another.'

Two different approaches

Staying with the issue of redundancy, consider the strategy of a company which is forced to close one of its factories. Alpha Martin are manufacturers of high-technology communications equipment. After several years of enviable prosperity and rapid expansion, sales have been hit by a competitive pincer movement, squeezing Alpha Martin on quality and price. The board decides to cut its losses by withdrawing from a section of the market. Redundancies are inevitable.

The success of the plan hinges on the co-operation of the workforce. After inconclusive negotiations, the managing director sets up two regional staff meetings with the aim of selling the package to the company as a whole. Since he cannot be in both places at once, the task is shared by the chairman of Alpha Martin, a bluff, no-nonsense character from the old school of management who believes in giving it to them straight.

The no-punches-pulled approach

Right then. I've called you together today to tell you what we've decided to do to put Alpha Martin back where it belongs—as the leader of our industry.

Now there's been a lot of gossip and rumour these last few weeks and I want to say, here and now, that most of the stories going around are entirely without foundation. You'd think people had something better to do than spread stupid tittle-tattle, but there it is.

Of course, we do have a few problems, as I'd be the first to admit. But they're problems we can solve without too much difficulty just so long as we're honest with ourselves and recognise why we got into this mess in the first place.

Don't misunderstand me. I am not about to start apportioning blame for what has happened. But I do think there is an important lesson to be learned. We cannot afford complacency.

To be blunt—and I know you wouldn't want me to pull my punches—there are too many people in this company who think all they have to do to earn a decent wage is to turn up in the morning. Well, it won't do. We need a fundamental change of attitude. Every one of you should leave this meeting today determined to make a greater effort. Alpha Martin has been good to you, now it's time for you to be good to Alpha Martin.

Very well. Let's talk about what else we have to do to get ourselves back into shape. First, we must cut costs.

And since the biggest cost we have to bear is labour, it follows, as night follows day, that some of our workers will have to go. I'll come back to that in a minute.

Along with the cutbacks in labour goes a cutback in certain areas of production where our rivals are giving us a hard time. As we all know, the new 244 has been a great disappointment. With sales well below forecast and no prospect of them picking up we have decided to cancel the entire project. As a result the factory at Handset will close and up to 300 jobs will go. I am naturally very sorry about this but there we are; we can't ignore the commercial facts of life.

Now, I know you won't want me to go into great detail about redundancies. Your area managers have all the relevant information and will be talking with you shortly if they have not already done so.

But there is one other vital point I want to make. The next year or two will not be easy. If the rescue plan is to succeed we must all dedicate ourselves to hard work. The time for automatic wage increases is over. The work must come before the rewards and not, as so often in the past, the other way round.

We can succeed. It is up to you.

That speech can fairly be described as a morale cruncher. The audience will depart with lower spirits than when they arrived, the very reverse of what the speaker intended. How did he achieve this unenviable distinction?

● He has not taken the trouble to think out what he really wants to say. This is evident from the inconsistency in the terms used about the company's state of health. What he describes as 'a few problems' hardly worth worrying about become, a few lines later, 'this mess', which demands radical action to sort it out.

● The patronising tone of the speech is calculated to fuel resentment. The offensive distinction between 'you' who are responsible for the crisis and who must therefore make sacrifices and 'us', by implication the innocent victims of so much bungling, fatally weakens the climax of the speech. It does not take a Freudian analyst to understand what the chairman is getting at when he declares, '*We* can succeed. It is up to *you*.'

● When the chairman is not patronising, he is hectoring. He may be right in believing that Alpha Martin is carrying too many shirkers and time-servers but this is not the occasion to labour the point.

● The structure of the speech is chaotic. So confused is the sequence of argument, the best lines for a peroration are thrown away in the opening seconds. How much more effective it would have been to end with the promise 'to put Alpha Martin back where it belongs – as the leader of our industry'.

● Having mentioned redundancy, he makes the fatal mistake of not following through ('I'll come back to that in a minute'). Now everyone is on tenterhooks, waiting for the blow. They are not in the least interested in anything else the chairman has to say.

● But the most serious failing is the chairman's apparent inability to project the future in any but the most mundane terms. Hard work and sacrifices are called for, but to what end? Restoring Alpha Martin to its former eminence is a recognisable objective but while the conditions for achieving this are forcefully proclaimed, it is not at all clear how this will affect employees and their families.

The speech is open to other criticisms (his gung ho delivery is not to everyone's taste, for example) but we have enough to be going on with. The question is, can Alpha Martin's managing director put in a much better performance, one that is strong enough to lift morale throughout the company?
    We'll see.

The counterbalanced approach

Good morning, ladies and gentlemen.

I've called this meeting to share with you a few ideas on how Alpha Martin might progress in the next stage of its development.

It has been a difficult and, in many ways, a frustrating year. There is no getting away from this sorry fact. But I must tell you that not once have I doubted our ability to win through. The reason for my confidence is plain to see. Alpha Martin has the advantage of a staff whose determination to work together for the greater good has outweighed all other considerations. For this, I thank you.

But we have some way to go before we can claim victory.

While we have succeeded in making substantial economies, the margin between profit and loss is still very narrow. This state of affairs puts the company in a dangerous position. Unless we can increase our profit ratio we will be unable to afford the research and development for the next generation of technology. This means we will come under increasing pressure from our competitors who, in the long run, could very well force us out of the market altogether.

Now, there is no reason why we should let this happen. And I, for one, have no intention of letting it happen.

What can be done?

Think of the market-place as a battle-field. Alpha Martin has suffered a punishing but by no means decisive setback. The only sensible course of action is a strategic withdrawal. We need to pull back from the fighting. Only then can we regenerate our strength for a fresh attack.

The most painful consequence of this manoeuvre is the loss of the 244. We would all wish it to be otherwise but if Alpha Martin is to survive to fight another day, I see no alternative.

We must face the fact that the 244 has not attracted the business we expected. This is not to blame any of those who have worked on the project. They have done their best in increasingly difficult circumstances.

But to go on losing money when resources are desperately needed elsewhere would be unfair on the rest of the company.

I am therefore recommending to the board that we stop production of the 244 forthwith and close our plant at Handset. As a result, 300 jobs will go.

I state this boldly because I do not want to disguise the seriousness of the position.

But there are some compensating factors which help to brighten up the picture.

First, up to 100 of our people at Handset—those who are within seven years of retiring age—are eligible for full pensions.

At least another hundred will be offered jobs in other parts of the company.

For the rest, we are making strenuous efforts to help them find alternative work. I am delighted to say that we have already had an encouraging response from Handset companies with immediate vacancies for skilled labour.

All of those leaving Alpha Martin, including those opting for early retirement, will be entitled to redundancy payments based on the number of years they have been with the company.

I want to make it absolutely clear that their departure in no way reflects badly on their work. All of us owe our colleagues at Handset a great debt of gratitude.

What, then, of the future?

The next year or so will not be easy. Even with the cancellation of the 244, we will need to marshal all our resources for the next attack on the market. If we succeed, then is the time for congratulations and the sharing of rewards. Until then I urge that we concentrate on the task in hand.

Let us leave this meeting determined to put Alpha Martin back into first place.

I dedicate myself to this goal. I hope you will join me.

Success! The managing director sits down to shouts of support and a well deserved round of applause.

These are his plus points:

- He started well with compliments to his hardworking staff and a message of encouragement—we can win through.
- He analysed Alpha Martin's problem clearly and succinctly and showed why the company had to restructure.
- When he delivered the bad news, the audience was ready for it.
- Having announced the cancellation of the 244 he immediately counterbalanced with news of what the company was doing to lighten the blow.
- His conclusion was a rallying call to inspire faith in the company and in its future.

The speech has four key components which together can shape a working model for all business people who have bad news to impart:

- **Why** is there a problem?
- **How** can we overcome it?
- **What** can we expect in return? (Counterbalance)
- **Where** do we go from here?

...And now the good news

It is not just bad news which can throw an organisation. Any announcement of radical change is disturbing and a potential source of conflict if it is not handled sensitively. This is so even when the change is intended to be wholly beneficial to everyone involved.

The continuing saga of Alpha Martin provides a typical case study. Returning two years after the crisis meetings on the cancellation of the 244, we find business picking up.

The general mood of optimism extends to the board room where the marketing director has put forward convincing arguments for an upward revision of his sales forecast. But to take full advantage of favourable market conditions, he recommends employing three more senior sales people. Agreeing to his proposal, the board instructs the personnel director to put out feelers for suitable candidates.

An announcement of the staff changes is scheduled for a forthcoming sales conference. But well before that event, a rumour leaks out of a major restructuring of the sales department. What is going on? If new people are coming in at the top, does this mean an end to the promotion hopes of those one level down the hierarchy? Is this the first move towards a shake-up of the department? If so, who will be the first to go?

By the time the sales conference comes round, many of those attending are thoroughly unsettled. At the same time, they are dying to hear what the marketing director has to say. Never before has he had such a receptive audience.

Fortunately, he knows that the framework for the delivery of bad news can serve equally well for the announcement of any major departures from the norm.

- **Why** is there a need for change?
- **How** is it to be implemented?
- **What** is the counterbalance?
- **Where** do we go from here?

The marketing director composes his speech accordingly:

This has been a good year. My congratulations to you all but particularly to our friends in the northern and north-eastern regions where there was a strong recovery after disappointing sales early on. Overall, we are 10 per cent ahead of forecast. This is quite an achievement, bearing in mind that just two short years ago we were slipping way behind our targets.

Now, at this stage of the game, it would be easy enough for me to announce a yet more ambitious sales forecast for next year and leave you to get on with it. Some of you might even relish the challenge. I can see that George is dying to get out there to show us all how to make a million.

But this would be too easy. For me, that is; not for George.

Why there is need for a change.

The fact is, Alpha Martin is entering a new phase of development in which we can expect sales to increase very substantially.

This is because the company is now in good shape to compete in sectors of the market previously closed to us. New products are coming on stream which I believe will catch the public imagination. Advertising and promotion budgets will match expectations of a major breakthrough.

With all this excitement it would be foolish for the sales department to stand still.

The priority, it seems to me, is to strengthen the sales force in a way that will enable us to take full advantage of the opportunities.

How is change to be implemented?

This is why I have recommended three senior appointments.

The first relates to the north-eastern region where the expansion of business justifies another sales manager. A second manager will be appointed to look after the south east—potentially a big growth area, which for too long we have treated like a poor relation.

Finally, I want to bring in someone to be in charge of sales training.

What can we expect in return?

Now, as I am sure you realise, the aim is to strengthen the sales department in preparation for the next stage of expansion.

Those of you in the front line will benefit greatly from an improved back-up service. I want to sort out the administration to give you more time to concentrate on what really matters—getting in the orders.

I need hardly add, if the plan works, there will be a corresponding gain in your earning power.

Where do we go from here?

In two years Alpha Martin has achieved a remarkable turnaround. Our targets for next year reflect our confidence in the future.

At previous meetings I have stressed our long-term objective—to put Alpha Martin back on top.

That is still the aim; only now I think we should stop calling it long term. The prize is in reach. It is ours for the taking.

No doubt before long the marketing director will be explaining other projected changes in the life of Alpha Martin.

An office move perhaps:

● **Why** are we moving?	We have outgrown our present accommodation.
● **How** will it happen?	A larger building has been acquired, some distance from the present site.
● **What** is the counter-balance?	More space. More pleasant surroundings.
● **Where** now?	The new building should take care of all our needs for the foreseeable future. So, make yourselves at home.

Or a merger with a rival company:

● **Why?**	To strengthen product development and marketing.
● **How?**	By bringing together certain administration functions.
● **What** is the counter-balance?	A chance to move forward more rapidly.
● **Where** now?	Into overseas markets in a big way.

Any change can be painful when it is not explained and promoted. Moreover, a good speech on behalf of change is better than a thousand written communications. How many notices are misinterpreted? How many are even read?

There are managers who argue that spoken and written words are equally liable to be misunderstood. The only way forward, they claim, is to move cautiously and silently. Change by stealth is their motto. It can work, in the long run. But as the man said, in the long run we are all dead.

4

The Telephone Training Session

Pity the training officer. While called upon to lead the way in fashioning the skills for the enterprise economy, few companies give him the money to do a decent job.

To compensate for the lack of staff and equipment, the training officer must exercise his imagination.

Take, for example, a primary business skill in which most companies are notoriously deficient—the use of the telephone. There are few office workers who would not benefit from telephone training and few companies in which telephone training would fail to enhance productivity. Yet there is little in the way of instructional material. A few enterprising training departments make their own videos but those who buy in courses can end up with an abominably produced multi-part series on telephone *selling*—a highly specialist activity favoured by commercial sharpshooters.

Faced with a demand for a session on telephone technique, what is a training officer to do?

What he does not do is deliver a formal lecture. With the best will in the world, the average student can absorb only a small proportion of uninterrupted speech: the figure has been put as low as 10 per cent. Given that training can sometimes be regarded as an imposition, an unnecessary extension of work (so many people think they know all there is to know about their jobs) the attention span may be even shorter.

To run a training session is to work hard at making the subject interesting. What are the possibilities?

- Good and bad ways of using the telephone can be demonstrated. The essential props are easily obtained and it does not take much electrical skill to fit up a system of bells and buzzers. So—don't just talk about how to use the telephone: show them.
- Telephone training is an ideal subject for role play. But to be effective, at least in the initial stages, role play must be supported by a script and by rehearsal. Volunteer actors summoned forward on the day cannot be expected to lead the session. The students' turn comes later.
- Instruction can be reinforced by humour. The awfulness of what passes for telephone conversation borders on farce. Without trying for an all-comedy show, the training officer should know that a few laughs help to stimulate interest.

Say the objective is to put together a session for newly recruited telephonists. They need to be shown that their telephone manner is critical to business and that mistakes can be very costly.

The training officer begins by collecting examples of telephone howlers. They come under three main headings:

- Lack of common sense.
- Lack of organisation.
- Lack of manners.

Now he writes some convincing dialogue to show what happens when these howlers occur. At this point it is easy to go over the top, to strive for dramatic impact by involving too many characters in an excessively complex plot. Resisting this urge, the training officer settles for the two characters— himself as presenter and customer and, at the receiving end, a receptionist cum sales assistant who will appear in various guises. Whoever plays the receptionist has to have enough acting talent to project different attitudes and voices. But she does not have to learn all her lines by heart. Given that for most of the session she will be seated behind a telephone, she can refer to a crib sheet while still managing a convincing portrayal. The training officer needs to be better acquainted with his material because, playing two roles, he must be ready to move about the set. But there is no reason why he cannot carry a script.

The scene is as simple as the action. There are two telephones, one at each end of the table. Both have bells which will ring on the press of a button. At one telephone sits the receptionist; at the other telephone stands the training officer.

The telephone training session is about to begin.

Incoming calls

TRAINING OFFICER:
How many of us realise, I wonder, that when this happens (phone rings) and we do this (picks up receiver), we are actually making use of the most powerful instrument of person-to-person communication the world has ever known. (Puts back receiver.) That also makes it the most powerful sales and marketing tool for just about any business you can mention.

Yet, in so many companies, the telephone represents, more than anything else, a succession of lost opportunities.

And why? Because the person in charge of the phone does not understand what it can achieve—for good, or, if badly handled, for ill.

(Turns towards receptionist)

Any messages, Miss Jones?

RECEPTIONIST:
Well, there was someone who rang. I think his name was Smith. He says his number is in the book.

(Someone offstage strikes a loud gong)

TRAINING OFFICER:
Any messages, Miss Jones?

RECEPTIONIST:
That awful man Simpson rang. He's

so rude. Anyway, I sent him off with a flea in his ear.

(Gong)

TRAINING OFFICER:
Any messages, Miss Jones?

RECEPTIONIST:
A Mr Robinson wants you to ring urgently. But he didn't leave a number.

TRAINING OFFICER:
It happens. It happens all the time. And if, as a consequence of these howlers, we lose business we have no one but ourselves to blame.

Here are a few more examples of bad practices. See if the cap fits.

(Training Officer now acting as a customer, picks up receiver and presses some numbers. Receptionist's phone rings.)

RECEPTIONIST:
Serve You Right Superstore.

CUSTOMER:
Good morning. Radio and TV department, please.

RECEPTIONIST:
Just putting you through.

(She does nothing, but just sits there. The customer is left on the end of the line looking exasperated. The receptionist leans forward and speaks in a slightly different voice.)

SALES ASSISTANT:
TV and Radio.

CUSTOMER:
Oh, there you are. Look, can you help me? I want to buy a Carry Component System.

SALES ASSISTANT:
That's a radio, isn't it?

CUSTOMER:
Radio and tape, yes.

SALES ASSISTANT:
I only do TV. You need Miss Western.

CUSTOMER:
(Wearily) I'm sure I do. Well, can you put her on?

SALES ASSISTANT:
She's at coffee break.

CUSTOMER:
Well, is there anyone else who can help me?

SALES ASSISTANT:
There's Mr Herbert.

CUSTOMER:
(Expectantly) Yes?

SALES ASSISTANT:
But it's his day off.

CUSTOMER:
Oh, forget it.

(Caller slams down phone.)

SALES ASSISTANT:
Have a nice day.

TRAINING OFFICER:
Well, at least she's polite. But the problem there is simply lack of organisation. It's no use inviting enquiries and orders by phone if there's no one around who can answer simple questions. And that's only one side of the story.

Let's see how it might have worked out if Miss Western—our radio expert—had been available to take the call.

(Both pick up their receivers.)

MISS WESTERN:
Hello, Miss Western speaking.

CUSTOMER:
Oh, Miss Western, I'm told you can
advise me. I want to buy a Carry
Component System.

MISS WESTERN:
We have quite a selection. Do you
know which model you want?

CUSTOMER:
Yes. And I have a reference number as
well. It's the CA-W5.

MISS WESTERN:
If you'll hold on a moment, I'll check
if there's one in stock.

CUSTOMER:
Thank you.

MISS WESTERN:
(Flicking papers) Yes, here we are. The
CA-W5.

CUSTOMER:
That's marvellous. And you have the
model in store?

MISS WESTERN:
Oh yes. There's no problem.

CUSTOMER:
In that case, if I give you a credit card
number, can you deliver for me?

MISS WESTERN:
Ah. Now that is a problem.

CUSTOMER:
Oh, why?

MISS WESTERN:
I don't know about delivery. I'll have
to ask Mr Jones about that. I know
it's all a bit difficult at the moment.
Couldn't you call in?

CUSTOMER:
(Sarcastically) I could. But that does

seem to lose the advantage of a delivery service.

MISS WESTERN:
(In hurt tone) Well, we do *try* to serve you right.

CUSTOMER:
So I discover.

(Both put down receivers.)

TRAINING OFFICER:
Not all the blame rests with the sales assistant. The management is equally at fault. But Miss Western should have been prepared for what is obviously a tricky question. And she needs to have her wits about her.

MISS WESTERN:
A credit card payment? Of course, sir. Which card do you wish to use?

CUSTOMER:
Access.

MISS WESTERN:
And the number?

CUSTOMER:
26714...

(They are interrupted by another call.)

MISS WESTERN:
One moment, please.

(She answers second call.)

Hello. Yes... Yes... The CR 27? Yes, it's ready for collection. Thank you. Goodbye.

(She goes back to the first caller.)

Sorry to keep you. I have all the particulars, don't I? There'll be a delivery next Thursday. Thank you. Goodbye.

(Customer looks surprised, but puts down his phone.)

Now where's that number?

(She looks through papers.)

Here we are. 26714 CR 27.

(Miss Western suddenly looks worried. She gives each phone a long look.)

Well! Isn't that a coincidence!

TRAINING OFFICER:
After that we can be sure of one thing. The accounts department will not be pleased.

Let's go back to the beginning and see how matters could have been handled more efficiently.

For a start, Miss Western needs to get herself organised. Everything she needs should be in easy reach. And she should have a pen and pad in front of her.

(The sales assistant does all this.)

Right. We're ready to go.

(Phone rings)

MISS WESTERN:
Radio and TV. Good morning. I'll just check for you.

(Second phone rings. Miss Western answers and mouths silently into the receiver.)

TRAINING OFFICER:
It's a classic problem. Two important calls at the same time. What can she do? There are several possibilities. For example...

MISS WESTERN:
I'm sure we can help you, Mr Smith. But I'm on another call just at the moment. Would you mind if I pass you over to one of my colleagues?

TRAINING OFFICER:
Of course, this is not always possible.
She may be the only sales assistant on
duty. What then? Well, she might
say...

MISS WESTERN:
Can you hold for a moment?

TRAINING OFFICER:
This is risky. There is nothing quite so
frustrating as hanging on at one end
of the line when you don't know
what's happening at the other. Human
nature being what it is, we assume the
worst—we've been cut off, the sales
assistant is inefficient, or, even more
irritating, that she is being
deliberately obstructive.

But Miss Western has at least one
other option.

MISS WESTERN:
I am on another call at the moment.
Could I ring you back in about five
minutes? If I could just take your
number...

TRAINING OFFICER:
Good for Miss Western. Now all she
has to remember is that she said she
would ring back in *five* minutes—not
half an hour, or tomorrow morning,
when it's too late anyway. Successful
business on the telephone is very
much a matter of organisation and
planning. The natural muddler is
always a disaster on the phone.

Let's try again. This time with a
different type of business.

(Customer picks up the phone. Once
again the receptionist has a jumble of
papers in front of her. Also a cup of
tea.)

RECEPTIONIST:
(In a high pitched whine) Quick
Service Garage.

CUSTOMER:
Good morning. My name is...

RECEPTIONIST:
(Brusquely) Hang on...

(She puts down phone, throws paper
about, to find eventually, a sugar
lump for her tea. She drops the sugar
in the cup and stirs reflectively.)

Yes?

CUSTOMER:
My name is Bartholomew. I want to
book in my car for a 26,000-mile
service.

RECEPTIONIST:
Bath what?

CUSTOMER:
I'm sorry?

RECEPTIONIST:
Name. You said it was Bath
something.

CUSTOMER:
Bartholomew. B — A — R...

RECEPTIONIST:
I know. (She pulls a face at the phone
to say don't get superior with me.)

Right then. We can't do anything this
week.

(She flicks through diary.)

CUSTOMER:
Oh, very well. Next week will do.

RECEPTIONIST:
No, we can't do next week either.

CUSTOMER:
(Impatiently) Aren't you supposed to
be the *Quick* Service Garage?

RECEPTIONIST:
Oh we are. Once we get your car we do
the service very quick.

CUSTOMER:
I'll bet you do. Never mind. I'll take
my business elsewhere.

(Both put down receivers.)

TRAINING OFFICER:
The temptation here is to get superior.
The receptionist is so obviously
lacking in the social graces. But it's
one of the great illusions to assume
that a good telephonist is someone
who talks posh. Not so. We don't have
to change our accents—just our
manners.

RECEPTIONIST:
(Much more politely) There's a dreadful rush on at the moment. It doesn't
look as if we have a space for about
two weeks. Is there anything wrong
with the car? Well, in that case, I'm
sure we can fix you up for a few days—
then do the rest of the job at the end
of the month. Would the 28th be all
right?

TRAINING OFFICER:
That's what it's all about—giving a
feeling of competence and
dependability.

And, of course, living up to that
reputation. Now, one more. This time
we go to the other extreme.

RECEPTIONIST:
(Very superior) Dickens and Askew.

CUSTOMER:
(Nervously) Oh hello. Is that Dickens
and Askew?

RECEPTIONIST:
(Wearily) Yes.

CUSTOMER:
The estate agents?

RECEPTIONIST:
Yes.

CUSTOMER:
I'm enquiring about the house in
Springfield Road.

RECEPTIONIST:
Yes.

CUSTOMER:
Well, how much is it?

RECEPTIONIST:
One moment. Let me see. Here we are.
It's on offer at 96,000.

CUSTOMER:
(Gasping) That much. Oh dear. Will
they come down?

RECEPTIONIST:
Oh, I shouldn't think so. It's an up-
and-coming area, you know. Prices are
rocketing. What were you thinking of
paying?

CUSTOMER:
About 60,000.

RECEPTIONIST:
(Aghast) Sixty thousand? Oh, well, if
you're going that low you'd be better
off looking for a maisonette. Or you
could try a cheaper area, where the
property is more run down.

CUSTOMER:
Where would you suggest?

RECEPTIONIST:
Somewhere like Northgate Street?

CUSTOMER:
But that's where I live now.

RECEPTIONIST:
And very nice, I've no doubt. Good
morning.

(They both put down receivers.)

TRAINING OFFICER:
Here we have the problem of the superior telephonist—the one who thinks she's got it made and treats the customer as if she's doing him a favour. She pops up quite often in successful businesses. But we all know that success in business is never guaranteed. None of us can afford to turn away customers. They deserve consideration.

All the characters portrayed here would do well to remember a few golden rules.

Here they are:

Your telephonist should have a pleasant and distinct voice.

RECEPTIONIST:
Good morning. Dickens and Askew. Can I help you?

TRAINING OFFICER:
She should not have an accent which is virtually incomprehensible.

(Receptionist repeats her Good Morning routine in gibberish.)

She should be polite and considerate.

RECEPTIONIST:
Yes, of course, Mr Jones, I do understand the urgency.
Unfortunately we are fully booked this week, but if you would like to talk to the supervisor...

TRAINING OFFICER:
Not impatient and ill mannered.

RECEPTIONIST:
All right, all right. You're not the only one with problems you know... Don't talk to me like that...

TRAINING OFFICER:
A telephonist needs to be cheerful and sympathetic.

RECEPTIONIST:
Hello Mr Jones. We haven't heard from you for some time. What? Oh, I am sorry. Anyway you're better now. Good. Well, what can I do to help?

TRAINING OFFICER:
But not over familiar.

RECEPTIONIST:
Mr Jones? Where have you been then? In hospital eh? Anything you can tell me about? A slipped disc? Hmmm. What have you been up to?

TRAINING OFFICER:
Brief and to the point.

RECEPTIONIST:
I'll just make a note of that. You want the order delivered to 45 St Stephen's Avenue some time this afternoon.

TRAINING OFFICER:
Not too long-winded.

RECEPTIONIST:
Well, I'll have to check that out. St Stephen's Avenue, you say. Is that the road down by the station? The one just after the roundabout?

TRAINING OFFICER:
Above all, the person in charge of the telephone should be intelligent and organised.

We are, after all, talking about one of the central figures in modern business. Someone who can make or break the company they represent.

The framework for this training session is highly adaptable. The sketches can be swapped about or given greater or lesser emphasis as circumstances dictate. Settings can be changed from one business to another with only slight amendments to the dialogue.

Just remember to leave plenty of time for questions and discussion—and for follow-up improvised role play.

Outgoing calls

Continuing with the example of telephone training, let us try the role-play technique with outgoing calls.

All the rules discussed so far—the need for a pleasant and distinct voice, friendly manners and so on—apply with just as much force here. In addition, there are the rules of procedure which have particular application to those who initiate telephone calls.

The distinction can be seen most clearly if we follow the progress of a salesman who is using the telephone to contact a likely prospect. This is an everyday occurrence for business people, including many who would not immediately think of themselves as part of a sales team. A managing director might want to follow up on a contact in banking to explore the possibilities of raising venture capital (he is, in fact, selling an idea) or a charity organiser might try to get through to a well known television personality (he wants to persuade the star to give his services to a worthy cause).

Whatever the motive, the circumstances of this type of call have one feature in common: A knows B slightly, if at all, but he hopes to use his vocal powers of persuasion to make closer acquaintance, usually by setting up a meeting.

The props are the same as in the earlier sketches but now we need three characters—the training officer doubling as presenter, plus a secretary and a salesman.

Another change is in the way the session is structured. This time, the training officer follows a clearly defined routine as sanctified by the gurus of sales practice.

TRAINING OFFICER:
First, take charge of the call from the very beginning.

Do *not* ask a secretary to get through to the number on your behalf. It may appear to save time to have someone else do the mundane work but if you are not fully concentrating on the task in hand the chances are you will not be ready to take over the call at the critical moment.

This can happen:

SECRETARY:
(After pressing some numbers) Hello, is that Mr Cowley? Good morning, Mr Cowley. I have Mr James on the line for you. Hold on just a minute, please.

(She presses the hold button and looks around wildly. Mr Jones is not at his desk. She goes back to the telephone.)

Hello, Mr Cowley. I am sorry but Mr Jones seems to have disappeared somewhere. Would you like to hold or shall I get him to ring you back? (She listens to some harsh words from the other end.) Oh, yes; of course. He was ringing you, wasn't he? Oh dear. I *am* sorry.

(She replaces the receiver looking very sheepish.)

TRAINING OFFICER:
Disaster! And thoroughly bad manners. To put through a call and then keep the person waiting at the other end of the line is to score an own goal in the first minute of the match.

Second, talk to a person by name not by job title.

A recipe for failure is to ask, say, for the personnel director and then have to rely on him to provide an identify.

SALESMAN:
(Talking into the receiver in a thoroughly confused manner) Oh, hello Mr Er Um. I wanted to talk to you. Yes, indeed. But we...

I'm afraid I didn't quite catch your name.

TRAINING OFFICER:
How insulting. There is only one proper response. 'So you don't know who I am. Well, if you want to talk to me about something important, I suggest you find out. Goodbye.'

It is the simplest thing in the world to check out the name of the person you want. Just ask the receptionist.

SALESMAN:
Good morning. Can you help me, please?

TRAINING OFFICER:
The answer to this question is always 'Yes'.

SALESMAN:
I want to contact the personnel director, but I'm not sure I have the correct name. Could you tell me what it is?

TRAINING OFFICER:
Or.

SALESMAN:
I'd like to talk to someone in the production department about a new computer-controlled assembly. Can you suggest whom I should contact?

TRAINING OFFICER:
The receptionist will invariably come up with the right answer.

Third, ask for whoever you want by his full name. 'I'd like to speak to John Smith, please.' Asking for Mr Smith could lead into a blind alley. 'Oh, you mean Mr Smith of personnel. I thought you meant Mr Smith of catering.'

Even uncommon names can be duplicated in such a large company.

SALESMAN:
Mr Cadwallider, please. (Pause)

Mr Cadwallider? (Looking puzzled)
That's funny, you don't sound like
Mr Cadwallider. (Hurriedly) Oh yes,
I'm sure you are Mr Cadwallider. But
are you the *real* Mr Cadwallider? No,
what I meant to say was... (Ends in
confusion.)

TRAINING OFFICER:
How much easier to have asked for Mr
Eric Cadwallider and saved all that
embarrassment.

Fourth, be wary of secretaries.

After the receptionist, the next person
you are likely to speak to is a
secretary. Proceed with great caution.

Most secretaries see themselves in the
role of holy protector. Their purpose in
life is to repel the unexpected caller
before they disturb the peace of the
inner office. Anticipating opposition,
perhaps even hostility, go in on the
attack. Fire off a direct question.

SALESMAN:
Is Mr Jones in?

TRAINING OFFICER:
The secretary might say, 'No, Mr
Jones is not in. Can I take a message?'

SALESMAN:
You might say that Michael Wilson of
Opportunities rang. But I think it
would be best if I tried ringing back.
Could you suggest a convenient time?

TRAINING OFFICER:
That's good. Once again, the secretary
is forced to make a constructive
response. She might say, 'He's out for
the day. But he should be available
early tomorrow morning. You could
try at about nine.'

This is a clear indication that secretarial opposition has been overcome. Come the next day, the caller is almost certain to be put straight through to Mr Jones.

Fifth, do not leave messages.

On no account try to persuade the secretary of the importance of the call. To understand why, imagine what happens when the invitation to leave a message is accepted. Remember, the caller has never met Mr Jones, who, in turn, has no idea what is required of him.

SALESMAN:
Thank you. Yes. I will leave a message. My name is Michael Wilson of Opportunities. We're in the business of helping middle managers adjust to the demands of the enterprise economy. I wanted to speak to Mr Jones because I'm hoping to persuade him... (Fade out)

TRAINING OFFICER:
Meanwhile, the secretary is thinking, 'Is this important enough to pass on to Mr Jones?' Because it is now evident that Michael Wilson knows Mr Jones only as a name on a contact list, the chances are that she will decide to give the message low priority. It may not even get to Mr Jones this side of Christmas. By falling for the temptation to leave a message, the caller has, in effect, talked himself out of the chance of setting up an early meeting.

Rule six: keep the initiative.

Unnecessary risks attend another routine offer of secretarial help. She might say: 'No, Mr Jones is not in, but can I get him to ring you back?'

To accept brings the inevitable follow-up.

SECRETARY:
Can I tell him what it's about?

TRAINING OFFICER:
At this point, the caller who is wise to the dangers of leaving protracted and—by the time they get through—incoherent messages may try to bluff his way through.

SALESMAN:
Just tell him it's Michael Wilson of Opportunities. I'd like to talk to him on a matter of some urgency.

TRAINING OFFICER:
This is highly risky. Mr Jones will return the call, there is no doubt of it, but when he finds out what it is all about, he may feel that he has been duped. The fact is that Mr Jones and Mr Wilson are highly unlikely to agree on what is urgent. 'I'm glad you think this is important, Mr Wilson, but I have a different order of priorities—and a very busy day in front of me. Goodbye.'

Rule seven: if the first call is unsuccessful, offer to ring back.

Let us return to the opening of the telephone conversation with the secretary. This time the answer to the question, 'Is Mr Jones in?', is a little more encouraging.

SECRETARY:
Yes, but...

TRAINING OFFICER:
There are many variations on what follows.

SECRETARY:
Yes, but he's in a meeting.

(Pause)

Yes, but he's on the other line.

(Pause)

Yes, but he's on his way out of the office and in a frightful hurry.

TRAINING OFFICER:
We have already decided that it is unwise to expect a contact to return the call. Almost as dangerous is for the caller to push his luck with a contact who clearly has his mind on more pressing matters.

SECRETARY:
Mr Jones is here but he has a meeting in two minutes.

SALESMAN:
That's all right. This won't take long.

TRAINING OFFICER:
Oh yes it will. In any case why allow Mr Jones the cast-iron excuse for cutting you off in mid-stream? 'That's all very interesting, Mr Wilson. But I really must go now. Thank you for calling. Goodbye.'

Rather than chance this rebuff, offer to call back at a more convenient time. Similarly, if Mr Jones is on another line, it is rarely sensible to hold on in patient expectation. Why waste precious minutes? Unless the secretary adds a helpful, 'He'll only be a few seconds', or 'He's just finishing a call', tell her that you will try again later.

All this can be very frustrating. But initial calls which fail to go beyond the secretary do have a value. The comfort is the knowledge that it is always easier second time around.

SALESMAN:
This is Michael Wilson. I rang earlier

but Mr Jones wasn't available. Is
there any chance I might speak to him
now?

TRAINING OFFICER:
Even that slight familiarity based on
a single earlier call helps to lower the
barrier of suspicion.

SECRETARY:
Yes, of course, Mr Wilson. Mr Jones is
free. I'll put you through.

TRAINING OFFICER:
Or she might say:

SECRETARY:
I'll check if Mr Jones is free. Can I ask
what it's about?

TRAINING OFFICER:
Resist the urge to say too much.

SALESMAN:
It's about the company training
programme.

TRAINING OFFICER:
That's all. Just enough to convince
the secretary that the matter to be
discussed is important enough to be
handled directly by the boss.

Now, our caller is within seconds of
his first break.

SECRETARY:
Mr Wilson? I have Mr Jones for you.

TRAINING OFFICER:
He's through!

Rule eight: get to the point quickly.

The secretary will have told her boss
who to expect when he picks up the
telephone. But never assume she has
got it right.

**Say immediately who you are and why
you are calling.**

SALESMAN:
Good morning. My name is Michael
Wilson of Opportunities. We specialise
in providing training programmes for
middle managers.

TRAINING OFFICER:
Never play games.

SALESMAN:
Hello there. We've never met but I'm
quite sure that when we've finished
this conversation you'll want to know
much more about my organisation and
the unique service we offer.

TRAINING OFFICER:
The recipient of this waffle may be too
polite to slam down the receiver—but
be sure that he has switched off long
before the caller has got to the point.

The opening dialogue with a contact
must contain an item of information
which commands his attention and
makes him want to hear more.

**There is no need to over-dramatise for
effect.**

'Our training programmes can save
you thousands of pounds' may be a
justifiable claim but sounds over the
top. Far better to opt for a more
modest assertion which none the less
impresses the listener.

SALESMAN:
I see from recent advertisements that
you are recruiting junior managers.
Our new training programmes are
geared specifically to their needs.

TRAINING OFFICER:
Perfect.

Having struck the right chord the
caller may feel encouraged to
continue. But remember this is not the
time for a full presentation. However

receptive the contact appears to be, it is nearly always wisest to stick to the original objective—to secure an appointment.

SALESMAN:
Yes, I would very much like to tell you more about our training programmes. Can I call on you some time next week?

TRAINING OFFICER:
At this point, the contact may draw back. The thought of squeezing another meeting into a crowded schedule is just too much. 'I'm really very busy at the moment. Can't you put some information in the post?'

Of course. And it may well be that promotional material will do the trick. But it is unwise to bet on it. The best advice is to persevere—to press just a little harder for a meeting.

SALESMAN:
I know how difficult it is to make time but I'll be very happy to come along early in the morning or late afternoon if that's easier for you.

TRAINING OFFICER:
An alternative ploy is to offer a choice between the particular and the general.

SALESMAN:
What about 9.30 on Wednesday or some time next week?

TRAINING OFFICER:
A contact finds it difficult to reject both without appearing downright rude.

The fixing of the appointment is the signal for concluding the telephone conversation.

SALESMAN:
Well, thank you Mr Jones. I look

forward to meeting you next
Wednesday at 9.30.

TRAINING OFFICER:
**The repetition of the date and time is
deliberate.** Let there be no misunder-
standings. In fact, to make doubly
sure, it is best to send a note of
confirmation along with any
introductory material.

There are those who favour a reversal
of this routine. They argue that an
introductory letter should precede any
telephone call. The virtue of this
approach is that a letter provides a
legitimate excuse for making a call.

SALESMAN:
Good morning, Mr Jones. I wrote to
you a couple of weeks ago from
Opportunities. If you have had a
chance to look at the material I sent
you perhaps we could meet to discuss
ways in which we might work
together?

TRAINING OFFICER:
While this is a perfectly good way to
start, it does assume that the initial
letter has made a favourable impact.
In practice, this is rarely the case.
This is because most business letters
fail to get across their essential
message.

But that is another story.

There we have an effective sales-training session which is in
no way dependent on audio-visual aids. Indeed, the intru-
sion, say, of a video on telephone techniques might even
weaken the instructional value of the session by distancing
the students from the main action.

The same formula can be used for many other areas of
training. Followed by open-ended discussion and improvised role play, it can bring enormous benefit at modest cost—
a training officer's dream.

5

Talking to the Media

Comes the time when a company attracts media interest, the managing director or his spokesman (usually whoever is in charge of public relations) will decide to call a press conference and to issue a statement.

When the message is easy

If the news is good—a successful takeover, say, or higher-than-expected profits or a new product to sweep the market—the statement causes little difficulty. Everyone agrees on what needs to be said.

> The directors of Span Holdings and Gale Enterprises are delighted to announce the success of their merger talks. The new company, to be known as S G Holdings, will be a market leader in the home and overseas markets. Plans for expanding production on a number of fronts will be announced shortly.

Having thrown in a few more generalisations, the managing director can sit back and invite questions, confident in the knowledge that the press will give him an easy ride.

When the message is difficult

But when the news is controversial or when the press conference is held in reaction to unfavourable reports of company performance, the problems begin.

For a start, *no one* can agree on what needs to be said. The result is an opening statement which, trying to accommodate all points of view, is so wordy and convoluted as merely to confuse the issue. Masters of the art of mystification were the old-style trade union leaders. There are still one or two around.

> In pursuance of resolutions unanimously approved by a majority of all branch committees, a specially convened meeting of the full executive being called to give comprehensive consideration to proposed action by the membership to restore the situation as it was before the company's unilateral abandonment of freely negotiated terms of employment, it was decided to adopt a non-cooperative relationship with the management in so far as this pertains to voluntary overtime.

Somewhere in thus guff is the threat of a strike. But the apparent reluctance to say so clearly immediately incurs the suspicion of the press. Who is hiding what? The hostile questions begin.

It is the same when a company tries to put across a justification for an unpopular action or an excuse for a disappointing performance. Instead of facing up to the challenge the tendency is to wrap up the central message in a thick coating of verbal fudge.

> I wish to say a few words about the scurrilous rumours that Span Holdings is in financial difficulty. Nothing could be further from the truth. As I need hardly remind you, it is an old established company with an enviable reputation for quality and fair dealing. We have survived many buffetings and I have no doubt we will survive many more. We have right on our side and the determination to win through.

> Finally, I would like to say just this ...

By now the media are as one in believing not only that Span Holdings is in trouble but that the chances of recovery are slight. In saying a lot about nothing, the Span managing director has given a strong, if unintentional, hint that he has a lot to hide.

How ironic that the confusion is created out of fear of what the press will do if they know the whole truth. Yet nine times out of ten, it is nothing to what they will do if they know only half the truth.

Assume that the managing director of Span Holdings has taken this lesson to heart. What then should he say to the press?

> Unexpected shifts in the value of the dollar and the consequent fall-back in some export markets have led to speculations about the financial health of this company.
>
> I can understand the concern while disagreeing with the analysis.
>
> A detailed breakdown of our trade figures over three years shows a shift in our export business from North America to Europe. The unfavourable exchange rate with the dollar will undoubtedly accelerate this trend.
>
> In the short run our sales abroad may not live up to the present forecasts. But I have no doubt that, in the longer term, the losses in the States will be more than compensated by increased business in Europe. Since this is entirely in accord with our long-range forecast, I see no immediate cause for concern.

This, you might say, is all very well. The managing director has a neat and logical response to his critics. But suppose there is no easy answer? Suppose the company really is in trouble and the management is having to face up to drastic remedies?

Even then it is wisest to come clean. To try to cover up

problems, when it is quite clear to independent observers that the problems exist, is merely to exaggerate their importance. The best advice is to acknowledge the bad news.

> We have had a tough year with turnover and profits down substantially.

Then immediately shift the debate on to more positive matters. What is to be done to solve the problems?

> We are mounting a programme of rationalisation which will lead to a leaner and fitter company. The first step is to cut our losses in North America by selling off our Detroit subsidiary. Negotiations are currently under way with several prospective buyers and I expect to announce a deal shortly.

Contrary to popular wisdom, the media are not obsessed by disaster. Journalists will nearly always report favourably on a businessman who takes a lead. This is not because the press is particularly high-minded in such matters. It is simply that a story about success, or success in the making, is far stronger than a story about failure.

The media will react badly to prevarication and dissembling. But who, apart from the liars and the cheats, would want it otherwise?

6

Welcoming a Foreign Delegation

British business has language on its side. The greater part of the world's commerce is conducted on our terms. If the Germans, the Japanese or even the French want to succeed in the international market, they must first learn English.

But this huge advantage can turn sour if familiarity with English leads to contempt for every other language. The businessman who subscribes to the threadbare clichés of cross-border communication (like talking loudly to anyone with an unfamiliar accent), may easily give offence and lose a deal. It happens all the time.

Make your welcome welcoming

To judge the British—and American—capacity for misleading foreigners, one has only to join the welcoming party for an overseas trade delegation. The red carpet treatment has to be lavish indeed to neutralise the impact of the typical speech.

> Now, before I start I just want to make sure: can everyone hear me? If you can't hear me, wave your hand. Like this. *That's* it. Well done, Sir. Now, does that mean you really can't hear me, or just that you can wave your hand? You *can* hear me? Good. Well, now we've managed to clear up that little matter, perhaps we can begin. First of all, on behalf of the

mayor and councillors of Mudwater, I
extend a felicitous welcome to you all.

As I'm sure you all know, Mudwater was
once a great centre of enterprise. I well
remember the days when the legend
'Made in Mudwater' was a guarantee of
quality. But, sadly, times change.
Nowadays, it is not enough to be proud
of our industrial heritage. We must face
up to the challenge of the microchip.

But facing up to the challenge is precisely what the speaker
has failed to do. He began by patronising his audience ('Can
you hear me at the back?') and then launched off on a defence
of the good old days, making it clear that if there was any
justice in the world, Mudwater would not be going cap in
hand to a bunch of foreigners.

Some guidelines
There is nothing for it but to start again, this time with a few
basic rules of hospitality.

- Make the visitors feel at home. When a Japanese car
  manufacturer came to the UK to choose a site for a new
  factory, the company president was delighted when a
  local reception committee presented him with a
  bouquet of his favourite flowers. He was less pleased
  with the administration of another enterprise zone, who
  could not even be bothered to get his name right. All
  else being equal, it is details like these that determine
  who comes out on top.
- The speaker should be able to identify all his guests by
  name and by job-title. Pronunciations need to be
  checked—and rehearsed. For the really difficult names,
  it can help to keep a note of phonetic spellings.
- A few words of greeting in the visitors' own language,
  even if they have to be learned by heart or read off a
  card, always meet with appreciation. There is no need
  to worry about stumbling over the grammar: it's the
  thought that counts. Just remember not to attempt so
  much that listeners start to assume linguistic skills
  which do not, in fact, exist.

● Skip the jokes. The British sense of humour can be
  irritatingly obscure to foreigners. Any sort of wordplay
  should be avoided. Puns are out. So too are jokey
  references to past battles. Jokey anecdotes about how
  father escaped from Singapore in 1942 are not likely to
  go down well with a party of Japanese. Why is it that
  even while trying to impress, some speakers feel
  compelled to settle old scores?

> I've always admired the Germans for
> their enterprise and industriousness.
> Of course, we've had our differences of
> opinion—quite violent ones I seem to
> recall—but, thankfully, the days of
> conflict are behind us.

Quite so. Then why mention them? The latest
generation of businessmen are too young to remember
the war and naturally resent barbed references to the
sins of their fathers.

● Local history can help to establish a bond between the
  visitors and their hosts. A little research may reveal
  examples of earlier commercial or cultural links which
  can be used to set the pattern for the future.
● Introduce everyone on the platform, say who they are,
  what they do and explain why they are there.
● Be clear about any unfamiliar social customs that may
  need to be observed. Remember that most other
  countries—including European countries—subscribe to
  a more elaborate pattern of formal manners.

For example, a speech of welcome to a party of Swedes
will inevitably draw a response from the leader of the
group. At a lunch or dinner, the words of thanks to
their host will come towards the end, whether scheduled
or not. It is wise, therefore, to plan for them, leaving a
suitable gap in the programme for the visitors to have
their say.

Case study: The Swedes

Remaining with the Swedes, imagine composing a speech of
welcome to a delegation of business people from Gothenburg.

We start with the advantage that the Swedes are wonderfully proficient in conversing in languages other than their own. But while anyone at executive level is likely to have a good grasp of English this is not to say that they follow all the nuances of an English business conversation—unless of course they have travelled widely, or lived here or in the States for some time.

The visitors from Gothenburg are on their first trip to Britain. Away from their home ground, they naturally feel a little uncertain as to what is expected of them. To overcome the famous Swedish reserve, they need reassurance and some tactful jollying along.

A good start is to check out information about Gothenburg. It is generally known that Gothenburg is the second city of Sweden, a busy port and the headquarters of several leading companies including Volvo.

It is less well known that Gothenburg has long-established commercial links with Britain. Indeed, at one time the city was known as Little London. There is more than enough here to be going on with.

Ladies and gentlemen,
welcome to Simpson and Goff, at this, the beginning of your tour of British boatbuilders.

I would like to be able to make this speech in Swedish but I'm afraid that my knowledge of your language is limited to a few words and phrases. That is my loss. However, I can at least get the name of your city right.

Phonetically:
Yerterborg

Gothenburg, I know, is really Göteborg. I do hope my pronunciation is correct. If not, we can blame

Erik Volien: group leader. The reference to him is made lightly, with a smile.

Erik Volien who rehearsed me earlier in the day.

That we have created our own way of saying Göteborg is an indication of the close business links between our two countries. I suspect that for us, Göteborg became Gothenburg when the first English and Scottish traders settled in southern Sweden in the seventeenth century.

It is one of the success stories of international commerce that those links have been strengthened over the years, not least in shipping and boatbuilding, an industry in which both our countries have a proud record.

Today, I hope to be able to give you an idea of how we at Simpson and Goff are facing up to the twin challenges of new technology and tougher competition, especially from the Far East.

We have a lot to cover in just a few hours. But you have an excellent guide in Steve Jones, who is sitting on my left. Steve is our production director and knows all there is to know about the new plant and its capacity for turning out quality products.

And so to the introduction of the rest of the team who will be participating in the day's programme.

After the welcome, and before getting into the swing of the occasion, it is a good idea to encourage the mood of easy informality by having everyone chat over coffee. It may seem a little early for a break but the aim, after all, is to make friends, and this is best achieved by direct contact. The business will follow naturally.

7

After-Dinner Speeches

The opening line

Good evening, ladies and gentlemen. It gives me great pleasure—but then it always has.

Why did nobody laugh? Well, for one thing, it is a very old joke, part of the stock in trade of every comedian. Then again, unless a speaker is absolutely certain of his audience, which virtually means knowing everybody by first names, it is a mistake to start with a risqué joke. Even a good one is more likely to provoke embarrassment than laughter.

So how does one launch into an after-dinner speech?

The first thing to be said is that while it is the time-honoured view that an after-dinner speaker (for which also read after-lunch speaker) should seek to entertain, it is not obligatory to keep up a barrage of rib-ticklers. If the organisers want unremitting humour, they should hire a cabaret act.

The ideal after-dinner speaker combines sensitivity and style. More than any other kind of speaker he must be aware of just how much his audience can take and be able to adapt accordingly.

While it is obvious that an excess of wining and dining reduces the attention span, this crucial fact rarely impinges on the content of an after-dinner speech. Having decided, say, to talk about the vagaries of economic forecasting, the honoured guest ploughs through a mass of detailed argument, unaware that his listeners have long since shut their minds to any questions more important than whether to order another brandy.

Yet even a subject as weighty as economic forecasting can be given a lift with the help of a little gentle humour. This is where the style comes in.

So often, it is not what is said that captures attention and raises a laugh but the way in which the material is put across.

> As you know, our chairman is a banker of some renown. I called in on him this afternoon to arrange an overdraft. He was very reluctant. But when I told him I was speaking this evening and made him listen to every word—by way of rehearsal, you understand—he suddenly became very reasonable. In fact, he promised me £100 for every minute I cut off my speech. (Tears up several pages.) That should see me through for the rest of the year.

As written, or indeed spoken, this is not the most hilarious story ever told. But put across with panache to a sympathetic audience (one that is not suffering from food poisoning), it will raise a few guffaws and establish a mood of easy entertainment.

> There are several accountants here this evening. You can easily spot them. They're the ones counting the silver.

Again, this is not what you might call a rib-cracker but it is strong enough to signal the intention of the speaker to keep cheerful. Economic forecasting can be fun.

If the self-made informal opener does not appeal, using someone else's words can achieve the same objective.

> 'A good accountant is someone who told you yesterday what the economists forecast for tomorrow.'
>
> *Sir Miles Thomas*
>
> 'If all economists were laid end to end, they would not reach a conclusion.'
>
> *George Bernard Shaw*

> 'Give me a one-handed economist. All
> my economists say: "On the one
> hand...on the other."'
>
> *Harry S Truman*

Any or all of these quotations offer a perfectly acceptable
way in to a speech on economic forecasting.

> Mr Chairman, ladies and gentlemen.
> You do me a great honour by inviting
> me to your annual dinner. You have
> asked me to speak about economic
> forecasting, an imprecise science if
> ever there was one.
>
> George Bernard Shaw hit the nail, I
> think, when he observed...

And off he goes.

But there is more to an after-dinner speech than a witty
opener. The good humour must continue to flow.

Some common errors

At this point it may help to put us in the right frame of mind
if we dispose of the more common sins of commission.

Tread carefully

It is so easy to cause offence. A joke that had them falling
about in the club can be received in icy silence by an after-
dinner audience.

A recent instance is Neil Kinnock's dig at the Prime Minister's renowned verbosity. Hearing a rumour that Denis
Thatcher had died, the BBC rushed an interviewer to Down-
ing Street. The press secretary was asked if Mr Thatcher
had spoken any last words. 'No, I don't think so', he replied.
'She was with him to the end.'

Now, it is easy to imagine the House of Commons bar falling about on cue, but when Mr Kinnock told the story at a
VIP gathering in Botswana, the response was less than
ecstatic. His audience of politicians and diplomats—those
who got the point—were embarrassed, while at home the
Opposition leader's political enemies had a field day with
their condemnation of sick humour.

Keep it clean
Resist sexist and racist jokes. This does not mean that a speaker must take a vow of puritanism, merely that he should draw a thick line between humour and vulgarity. The earlier warning against risqué jokes, for example, does not exclude any mention of sex. The ever-interesting topic is also an everlasting inspiration for sharply amusing observations on the human condition.

The indomitable Mae West had the right idea:

> 'I do all my writing in bed; everybody knows I do my best work there.'

> 'Save a boyfriend for a rainy day, and another in case it doesn't rain.'

> 'A man in the house is worth two in the street.'

> 'To err is human, but it feels divine.'

> 'It's not the men in my life that counts—it's the life in my men.'

> 'When I'm good, I'm very good. But when I'm bad I'm better.'

> 'It isn't what I do but how I do it. It isn't what I say but how I say it. And how I look when I do it.'

While we're at it, here are a few more notable one-liners which take the seriousness out of sex.

> 'It's the good girls who keep diaries; the bad girls never have the time.'

> 'I'm as pure as the driven slush.'
>
> *Tallulah Bankhead*

> 'Do you believe all the sex and violence in the movies today? Of course, at my age, sex and violence are the same thing.'

> 'There's nothing wrong with making love with the light on. Just make sure the car door is closed.'
>
> *George Burns*

> 'They say that drinking interferes
> with your sex life. I figure it's the
> other way around.'
>
> *W C Fields*

All good clean fun.

Be brief
Long-winded stories are definitely out.

For reasons that are inexplicable even to the chief offenders, after-dinner speakers are beset by the desire to savour the details.

> I well remember a young colleague of
> mine, let's call him Ben. This wasn't
> his usual name, of course. But I
> wouldn't want to give too much away.
> Well, at the time I knew him, Ben was
> in his late twenties, or maybe early
> thirties. Certainly not more than
> thirty-two or three. Anyway ...

By the time we get to the punchline, if there is one, it will be soggy as a sponge pudding. The antidote to long-windedness is rehearsal and yet more rehearsal. There is a tendency to think of anecdotes and funny stories as old friends, whose dependability is beyond question. But to get away with a story as part of a free-for-all conversation is not the same as telling it to an audience. The higher standard of performance can only be achieved by cutting out the extraneous words and phrases.

No dogs
Shaggy dog stories are debarred under the previous rule, and on two other counts. They are rarely funny — but even when there is a strong punchline it is too easy for an unpractised speaker to lose his thread. It is not unknown for a would-be comedian to miss the point of the joke altogether — and to be unaware of his error until later when he asks why nobody bothered to laugh.

Don't copy the experts
To imitate the techniques or plagiarise the material of professional humorists is to court disaster.

Just because Ken Dodd can bring an audience to the point of hysteria by waving a feather duster does not mean that anyone can work the trick. Even a professional mimic falls some way short of the real thing.

The hazards of plagiarism are most in evidence when an entire sketch is purloined. A frequent example is Alan Bennett's wonderful caricature of a Church of England parson, first heard over 25 years ago in the review *Beyond the Fringe*. Since then thousands of after-dinner speakers have tried to measure up to the Bennett talent for affectionate parody. It is a fair bet that the vast majority have failed embarrassingly.

Verse—and worse
The humour to be squeezed from comic verse is in inverse proportion to its length. Rambling poems are not appreciated, least of all when they are of the homespun tum-te-tum-te-tum variety.

Having identified the bear traps we can more easily map out the path towards the successful after-dinner speech.

Source material

Anthologies
Finding material—humorous or otherwise—is not difficult if you know where to look. A good place to start is with a book of quotations. Of the latest and best are the Bloomsbury *Dictionary of Quotations* and the Routledge *Dictionary of Quotations*. Both books are arranged by theme—from Absence and Abstinence through to Yielding and Youth. This makes for easy reference and is a vast improvement on the old-style compilation like Benham and Bartlett where the entries are listed by author.

Of the more specialist volumes the Chambers *Book of Business Quotations* takes a lot of beating.

By way of example of what can be gleaned from these anthologies, here is a random selection of quotes which could be worked in to virtually any speech on business or management.

'No nation was ever ruined by trade.'

Benjamin Franklin

'Everyone lives by selling something.'

Robert Louis Stevenson

'If I see something I like, I buy it;
then I try to sell it.'

Lord Grade

'Nothing is illegal if one hundred
businessmen decide to do it.'

Andrew Young (American politician)

'Business underlies everything in our
national life, including our spiritual life.
Witness the fact that in the Lord's
Prayer the first petition is for daily
bread. No one can worship God or love
his neighbour on an empty stomach.'

Woodrow Wilson

'Half the time when men think they
are talking business they are wasting
time.'

Ed Howe (American writer)

'The trouble with senior management
to an outsider is that there are too
many one-ulcer men holding down
two-ulcer men's jobs!'

Duke of Edinburgh

'Executive ability is deciding quickly
and getting somebody else to do the
work.'

J G Pollock

'Too bad all the people who know how
to run the country are busy driving
cabs and cutting hair.'

George Burns

The humour section of any bookshop contains a wealth of
material. Avoid the awful joke books in favour of the off beat.

Cartoon captions can translate well into sharp and pithy anecdotes.

With apologies to Hector Breeze	Two down-at-heel matchsellers are standing by the roadside. One is saying to the other 'I hate to think what it would be like if I hadn't been to Business School.'
With apologies to Herman	A boss addressing a line-up of hopeful looking executives: 'I'm sure you three will be pleased to hear I'm agreeing to your 15 per cent pay demand. 5 per cent each.'
With apologies to ffolkes	Psychiatrist to patient on couch: 'Of course you're depressed. I'm very expensive.'

One of the few humorous poets to lend himself to selective quotes is Ogden Nash, a stalwart of the *New Yorker* in the pre-war years. Nash had a penchant for invented words, which should be avoided. But his observations on the business and social life in New York are as fresh today as when he was writing in the 1930s.

> Most bankers dwell in marble halls.
> Which they get to dwell in because
> they encourage deposits and
> discourage withdralls.
>
> And particularly because they all
> observe one rule which woe betides the
> banker who fails to heed it.
>
> Which is you must never lend any
> money to anybody unless they don't
> need it.
>
> From 'Bankers Are Just Like
> Anybody Else, Except Richer'.

Humour books aimed at particular professions quickly suffer from over-familiarity but if they are new on the shelves they are certainly worth dipping into.

Recently, publishers who like to address colleagues on the state of their trade were blessed with the appearance of Bizarre

Books. Here in a single volume was encapsulated the lunatic fringe of the book business. To illustrate the infinitely varied nature of publishing or, conversely, to argue that some books are a waste of forest acreage, the speaker has only to refer to Bizarre Books. Their weird but not so wonderful titles include *The Biochemists' Songbook, How to Boil Water in a Paper Bag, One Hundred and One Ways of Spelling Birmingham* and—the autobiography of Dr Victor R Small—*I Knew 3000 Lunatics.*

Best served for specialist humour are politicians, doctors and lawyers, though why these professions should be so inherently funny is difficult for an outsider to determine.

Oxford University Press has done a great service to public speakers by publishing *Political Anecdotes* (Ed Paul Johnson) and *Legal Anecdotes* (Ed Michael Gilbert). No doubt a volume for the medics is in preparation.

As an indication of the riches to be found in the Oxford anthologies, here is that marvellous exercise in one-upmanship as performed by F E Smith (later Lord Birkenhead) when he was a young barrister. It is a touch on the long side but, with appropriate pauses, it can produce a succession of laughs, each greater than the last.

His worst insults were reserved for Judge Willis, a worthy, sanctimonious County Court Judge, full of kindness expressed in a patronising manner. F E Smith had been briefed for a tramway company, which had been sued for damages for injuries to a boy who had been run over. The plaintiff's case was that blindness had set in as a result of the accident. The judge was deeply moved. 'Poor boy, poor boy,' he said, 'blind. Put him on a chair so the jury can see him.'

F E said coldly: 'Perhaps Your Honour would like to have the boy passed round the jury box.' 'That is a most improper remark,' said Judge Willis angrily. 'It was provoked,' said F E, 'by a most improper suggestion.'

There was a heavy pause, and the judge continued: 'Mr Smith, have you ever heard of a saying by Bacon—the great Bacon—that youth and discretion are ill-wed companions?' 'Indeed I have, Your Honour; and has Your Honour ever heard of a saying by Bacon—the great Bacon—that a much-talking judge is like an ill-tuned cymbal?' The judge replied furiously: 'You are extremely offensive, young man,' and F E added to his previous lapses by saying: 'As a matter of fact we both are; the only difference between us is that I'm trying to be and you can't help it. I have been listened to with respect by the highest Tribunal in the land and I have not come down here to be browbeaten.'

He had a particular objection to a judge saying that he had read his case and thought little of it. One such judge said to him: 'I have read your case, Mr Smith, and I am no wiser now than when I started.' 'Possibly not, my Lord, but far better informed.'

Earl of Birkenhead, *F. E.*, 1959.

Biographies

Biography is full of riches. Inevitably there is an element of pot luck but selections can be made easier by looking to those who are known for their style and wit. The aphorisms of Oscar Wilde are mostly over-familiar but George Bernard Shaw, Max Beerbohm and G K Chesterton, to choose at random, can still turn up fresh and funny observations on every subject under the sun. Churchill and Lloyd George stay ahead for political anecdotes (even if many of them are apocryphal) while in show business every trip down memory lane is a discovery of quotable yarns.

The greatest gift to after-dinner speakers is the one-line joke, an art form of which the American writers and actors are the undisputed masters. Leading the field are Woody

Allen, George Burns, Bob Hope, Mel Brooks and, posthumously, Dorothy Parker, Groucho Marx and W C Fields.

'She's afraid that if she leaves, she'll become the life of the party.'

'There's one way to find out if a man is honest: ask him; if he says yes, you know he is crooked.'

'I didn't like the play, but then I saw it under adverse conditions—the curtain was up.'

'I never forget a face, but in your case I'll make an exception.'

'I'd horsewhip you if I had a horse.'

'The husband who wants a happy marriage should learn to keep his mouth shut and his checkbook open.'

'If you've heard this story before don't stop me, because I'd like to hear it again.'

'I'm 42 round the chest, 42 round the waist, 96 round the golf course and a nuisance around the house.'

Groucho Marx

'Once during Prohibition, I was forced to live for days on nothing but food and water.'

'I gargle with whiskey several times a day and I haven't had a cold in years.'

'Horse sense is what a horse has that keeps him from betting on people.'

'The best cure for insomnia is to get a lot of sleep.'

'I never worry about being driven to drink, I just worry about being driven home.'

'What contemptible scoundrel stole the cork from my lunch?'

'The cost of living has gone up
another dollar a quart.'

'My illness is due to my doctor's
insistence that I drink milk, a whitish
fluid they force down helpless babies.'

'After two days in hospital, I took a
turn for the nurse.'

'If at first you don't succeed, try, try
again; then quit—there's no use being
a damn fool about it.'

'I never drink water—I'm afraid it will
become habit-forming.'

'The world is getting to be such a
dangerous place, a man is lucky to get
out of it alive.'

W C Fields

Newspapers

Check out the diary columns of the better newspapers, in
particular Peterborough of the *Daily Telegraph* and Observer of the *Financial Times*, both of which end with a quotable paragraph—the latest City joke or a Freudian misprint
from the provincial press.

Heard in a Birmingham factory:
'Business is certainly picking up—
we're back to being two months
behind with our orders.'

Sign in the window of a Fulham shop:
'For sale cheap, as new electric guitar
and powerful amplifier. Phone... If
boy answers, please ring off and call
later.'

From a company staff magazine: 'The
sudden fierce gust of wind took all
who were at the ceremony completely
by surprise. Hats were blown off, and
copies of the chairman's speech and
other rubbish were scattered all over
the site.'

Other people

There are speakers, the natural raconteurs, who have their own private collections of stories to amuse. They go through life looking out for curiosities of behaviour which later might come in handy for arguing a point.

Cutting back on expenditure is a painful process. But the pain is not always shared equally. I remember once, my chairman sent me a stern memo calling for all senior managers to clamp down on unnecessary spending. It was written on Concorde notepaper.

George was one of the old school of businessmen who had to have his own way. On one of the rare occasions he was outvoted by his fellow directors, he went ahead anyway. The secretary duly noted in the board minutes: 'Resolution carried by a minority of one.'

George had as many enemies as friends—and he treated them both the same. His love of a good fight, without the benefit of Queensberry Rules, must have concerned his wife because when he died, she asked the clergyman if he thought George would be admitted to Heaven. 'Have no fear,' he replied judiciously. 'By now I suspect he has gained a controlling interest.'

It took a month to work out a strategy. Then, having got it typed up and in a smart presentation folder, he leaves it in the back of a taxi. Of course, it was the only copy. Our top-secret plan for survival. A couple of days later the precious document was returned in the post. With it was a polite note from the taxi driver saying that the figures on page two didn't quite add up. He was right, too. If I'd

have known who he was I'd have
offered him a job. But I suspect he
would have been too expensive.

All true stories. Well, true enough to serve their purpose in
an after-dinner speech.

Case study: Serious business

There is an obvious risk of giving so much attention to the
comedy routine that any serious message—assuming there
is one—gets carried away on a wave of laughter. The only
way to avoid this is to ensure that the core of the speech has
enough dramatic force to match the accompanying humour.

This is not as difficult as it may appear. The secret is to
present a subject, however familiar, in a way that will grab
the attention of the audience. Think of it from the point of
view of a businessman invited to speak at a chamber of commerce dinner on the touchy subject of business ethics. It
would be easy enough for him to take the standard line; that
we must all do our best by the public and by our employees,
not forgetting the primary rights of the shareholders and
the sanctity of the profit margin. His listeners would listen
politely, stifle their yawns and applaud dutifully—while
relegating every word of the speech to the memory shredder.

But suppose our businessman tries a little harder? What if
he raises a few pertinent questions about the way managers
interpret their responsibilities—and suggests a few changes?

Whenever I am invited to speak on
business ethics, I begin by asking
myself why this subject has been
chosen above all others.

There are several possible
explanations.

The unlikeliest is that the organisers
feel I know more about this subject
than any other.

Said tongue-in-
cheek.

Unlikely, because it is a well-known
fact that my expertise spreads far and
wide. Why can't someone ask me to
talk about bee keeping—or vintage

wines—or, even, what I did on my last holiday? All lively topics for discussion, I assure you.

The contrary argument—that I know *less* about business ethics than any other subject—could be a stronger reason for getting me along. When I told a friend what I was doing this evening, he was quick to draw a conclusion. 'So you're talking about business ethics,' he said. 'Well, at least the speech will be a short one.'

But I'm not so modest as to agree with that observation.

Rather, I would argue that we are all interested in business ethics because we have a natural desire to conduct our affairs in a way that is decent and honest. In the present climate it is not easy to reconcile economic probity with economic gain. Thus, business ethics is pushed to the forefront of public debate. We need to find some answers.

And why me to speak on this vital matter? Well, maybe it's because I am thought to have strong views. If this is the case, I will try not to disappoint you.

Let me start by telling you what I do not propose talking about. Discussions about business ethics often centre on such topics as staff welfare, product safety and responsibility for the quality of the environment. But not today.

While I do not want to understate the importance of these matters, they also seem to me to be secondary to other more fundamental problems which must take priority.

I am thinking of the scandals of insider trading, asset stripping, tax avoidance and all the other sharp, get-rich-quick fiddles that plague the business community.

That these devious practices are frequently undertaken by otherwise honest people is a fair indication of how far we still have to go to achieve a sound ethical basis for modern business.

In my view, there are four single principles which, if followed rigorously, would go a long way towards resolving the ethical dilemmas of business competition.

First, there is the principle of full disclosure. Anything that can be completely disclosed without embarrassment is inherently ethical. There is no exception to this rule.

The obverse is not necessarily true, however. Business competition involves secrecy and surprise, and something that must be kept secret is not necessarily unethical.

The proper instinct is to disclose unless there are good reasons for not disclosing. So many companies adopt the reverse procedure. Their first impulse is to keep everything under wraps and to release quite harmless information only under pressure.

I once came across a firm which made it the custom to use a red 'highly confidential' folder to circulate the memos for the directors' dining room.

Such obsessive secrecy is the natural ally of dishonesty and sharp practice.

Second, any profit gained from the unethical act of someone else is itself unethical—even when this occurs in good faith. A good example is the commission fee paid to a third party for fixing up a business deal. Where the fixer is taking money for a recommendation, this should be known to all parties involved. One sure way to find out is to insist on the disclosure option. If someone asks for a finder's fee I can ask him for a letter from his client authorising him to collect such a fee.

Third, it is unethical to betray the trust of those whose interests we represent. This can raise problems when the interests of employer or client come up against our own personal beliefs.

Suppose, as a committed anti-smoker, I find that my company is forging links with the tobacco industry? How do I react?

What I must not do is to fudge the issue, to think that I have the right to perform a job badly because it doesn't happen to fit in to my scheme of things. If I feel strongly about some aspect of policy, I should act accordingly—even to the extent of departing to more congenial employment.

Finally, there is the catch-all business principle. Anyone who believes in and profits by the free-market system is honour bound not to undermine it. This rules out collusion with business rivals, for instance. Also, the denial of opportunities to others on grounds of race, gender or creed.

It is my conviction that these principles should be taught in schools—and I do not mean simply in the business schools.

But it is not too late for the rest of us. It is the responsibility of us all to think

> about the ethics of business—and to
> realise that we are accountable not
> only to customers and colleagues—but
> to our own consciences.

That should get them thinking—and talking.

Case study: Talking to a lay audience

The problem of holding the attention of an after-dinner audience is accentuated when a specialist is called upon to talk to a lay audience. It is so easy to cause confusion by assuming too much knowledge or resentment by assuming too little. The speaker must see himself in the role of teacher, able to put over complex ideas in a way that can be generally understood.

Here is a professor of engineering addressing a group of finance and business people. We join him at the point in his speech when he is building up to talk about macro-engineering, a term which is new to most of his listeners.

> In macro-engineering we study the
> largest technological undertakings of
> which man is capable.
>
> Let me give you some examples.
>
> Before long, the space programme,
> that costly venture shared by the
> United States and the Soviet Union,
> will begin to pay its way.
>
> A powerful spacewatch camera will
> soon be able to identify asteroids with
> commercially useful minerals. Within
> the decade, a programme of space
> industrialisation may include the
> mining of the asteroid belt.
>
> Future demands for energy could be
> met by taking power from the sun.
> Orbiting reflectors could beam power
> to earth via microwave. The only
> deterrent for any one nation is cost,
> but at international level, the project
> becomes realistic.

Vast areas of arid land throughout the world could be made productive if they were supplied with water.

The concept of large-scale irrigation is nothing new. Indeed, no modern state has emulated the Romans in halting the northward advance of the Sahara Desert with a huge complex of aqueducts and tree belts.

Today, a canal system linking the main rivers of India would serve as a reliable source of irrigation for the entire subcontinent.

The irrigated land of North Africa could be doubled by a submarine aqueduct, in the form of a plastic duct, carrying water from the Rhone river under the Mediterranean and by canal over the Atlas mountains.

The future of transport is not in the air or on the ground. It is underground, by super-fast trains. Since they will travel without noise, be more economical on fuel and will not create pollution, they are likely to gain sympathetic support from the environmentalists.

There are already trains that can move at speeds in excess of 300 mph. Before long, supersonic speeds will be practicable.

In Japan they have a test track for an electromagnetically levitated train which, if introduced on a cross-channel run, could provide a one-hour service between Paris and London. The next step is to develop a wheelless train in a tube from which the air has been partially pumped out. Levitated tube transport, at supersonic speeds, will almost certainly be demonstrated within the decade.

As for the boring of the tunnels, the Japanese are completing the longest railway tunnel—33.46 miles. This makes our own Channel Tunnel, first mooted in 1751, a relatively minor enterprise.

Before long, we can look forward to an Atlantic tunnel. The only technical reason why this is not an immediate practicality is that no one has made a reliable map of the sea bed. The actual tunnelling presents no serious problems. After all, pipelines have been constructed at much deeper levels. The laying of the Atlantic cable goes back to the 1850s—an engineering feat that was far more impressive in those days than an Atlantic tunnel would be in our times.

Eventually there will be a tunnel system to provide high-capacity transport links with trading partners throughout the world.

We are on the verge of a dramatic evolution extending human habitation to man-built islands in the oceans. Fixed platforms are now commonplace in depths exceeding 600 feet and floating docks of considerable size are in use in Hong Kong and Japan.

Artificial islands for offshore mining to the outer limits of the continental shelf are a real possibility. In the same way, sea cities could be built in the shoal waters that constitute at least 10 per cent of the surface of the ocean.

If macro-engineering can contribute so much to human welfare, why does it arouse public and political hostility?

The first serious obstacle is the inherent suspicion of new and radical ideas.

This is where the environmentalist and conservation lobbies gain their strength. They would have us believe that we are all under threat from powerful businessmen and over-ambitious politicians who, given a free hand, would soon deprive the world of its essential resources.

They agree with Schumacher that 'small is beautiful'. But they take the Schumacher argument for small and intermediate technology too far. Schumacher did not condemn large-scale technology out of hand. 'It depends,' he said, 'on what you are trying to do.'

Thus, we can acknowledge the social and cultural problems caused by some massive building projects without dismissing brave attempts to create new towns and cities.

It is not simply with the advantage of hindsight that we acknowledge, say, the social and cultural waste of tearing apart city centres in the Fifties and Sixties to make way for charmless tower blocks. At the time, engineers were warned of the risks. That they were ignored tells us not so much about the awful effects of large-scale construction (in the right circumstances tall buildings can have enormous advantages), as about the failure of engineers and politicians to connect.

Even when they do try to get on, their efforts founder on mutual misunderstanding. The trouble is the two sides speak different languages. The result is a repetition of committees—yet another set up to examine the conclusion of the last—and a pile of unread reports.

Maybe what we need are schools of engineering diplomacy. They could teach presentation, promotion—all aspects of communication—including public speaking.

Somehow, we must get over to the politicians—and the voters—the exciting possibilities of the new engineering systems—on land, at sea and in space.

If we delay, future generations may come to know us as the age of failed imagination.

By now even the most self-indulgent dinner guest will have forgotten all about trying to catch the eye of the wine waiter. His full concentration will be on the speaker. What a fascinating man! What a profound thinker! We really must get him back to talk to us again.

8

The Role of Chairman

Early on we had some hard things to say about chairmen who misinterpret their brief.

It is *not* the job of a chairman to:

● Upstage the main speaker by stealing his material.

> In welcoming Mr Jones to this conference I must tell you that as we arrived this morning he made the most fascinating observation...

It was probably the centrepiece of his speech.

● Ramble on at great length about matters that do not relate to the subject in hand.

> Before we start, I would like to make a few announcements about next year's programme...

The longer he goes on, the louder the yawns.

● Downgrade the speaker.

> We were hoping to persuade the Minister to address us but he has to be at a Cabinet meeting so he has sent his parliamentary private secretary...

or:

● Oversell the speaker.

> For sheer charm, intelligence and wit Mike Jones is hard to beat.

At least, he is when he is not dying of embarrassment.

The chairman needs all the skills of the public speaker and then some.

Introductions

His introduction should be brief and to the point. He must remember that the audience is not there to listen to his views. At the same time they appreciate a brief warm-up session which helps set the tone of the meeting.

But the introduction is chiefly a service to the guest speaker. When it comes to his turn he wants to get straight into his subject. He does not want to waste time, and the patience of this audience, by having to justify himself as a person worth listening to.

Imagine the awkwardness of launching into a speech without the backing of a good chairman.

> Good evening, ladies and gentlemen. My name is Mike Jones. As some of you may know, I am managing director of Pax Engineering and I am here to talk about ways in which industry can revive levels of productivity.

What a tame beginning. But allowing for the probability that there are several in the audience who know nothing of Mike Jones, he has to establish his credentials. Maybe he should try to inspire interest with a few more claims to fame.

> I am chairman of this and that committee. I have travelled the world to address conferences of eminent business people and my wife was recently elected to the European Parliament.

But a recital of achievement sounds at best like special pleading and at worst like an attack of megalomania.

The intercession of a chairman can save the day. Assumed by the audience to be strictly impartial (he hardly ever is, but the convention is all) he can say nice things about the speaker without seeming defensive or boastful. If he pitches his introduction at the right level (more than an announcer but not quite a cheerleader) he will create for his listeners the expectation of an inspiring hour ahead.

> Good evening, ladies and gentlemen.
> I am delighted to welcome you to
> what I know will be a stimulating/
> thought-provoking session/lecture/
> talk.

If the chairman does not know the speaker except by vague reputation he may feel inclined to hedge his bets.

> No doubt, we will have an enjoyable
> evening.

Or

> I do hope we will enjoy an interesting
> talk.

But the cagey introduction sets up too many doubts. Who is this man? Is he really worth hearing? The chairman has a duty to back his speaker without promising the earth. If he is genuinely worried about the way the speech will be received, he should stress the virtue of constructive argument. The chairman who holds out the prospect of 'a stimulating evening' is on fairly safe ground.

Even if the speech arouses unanimous opposition, it will at least have 'stimulated' a reaction.

Anticipating a stormy session, the chairman does have the option of pitching in with a more forceful introduction which stresses the case for giving the speaker a fair hearing.

> There is no more emotive subject than
> the education of our children. But
> while I would not disguise from you
> my own sense of shock at the news of
> the imminent closure of our village
> school, I have to remind myself that
> there are always two sides to every
> question.
>
> Before deciding on action, we have a
> responsibility to examine the reasons

why the local authority has chosen this course. To put the education committee's point of view, I am very pleased to welcome James Elliott, the county's director of education. Mr Elliott is a hardy campaigner for improved standards in schools. He is, I know, entirely frank and honest in his views. I ask you to listen carefully to what he has to say and to save questions and comments for the end of his speech when there will be plenty of time for debate.

By contrast, introducing Mike Jones and his talk on productivity is an easy task. The goodwill of the audience can be assumed.

Let us start again with Mike Jones. His chairman needs to get over a few basic facts.

Mike Jones is known to you all as the managing director of Pax Engineering, a company he has led from recession to record profits.

Maybe. Not all the audience will be aware of Mike Jones and his triumphs but they will accept that they ought to know. Following these opening words, they will be keen to hear what he has to say.

This notable achievement has made him the natural choice for the chairmanship of the Productivity Council, the agency set up to advise industry on making better use of its resources.

And it is on this very subject that we have invited Mike Jones to talk to us today. It would be difficult to think of anyone better qualified to take on this challenging theme. (Turning to the speaker)

You have a ready audience, Mr Jones. We eagerly await your speech.

The speaker is duly launched. Off he goes with some pertinent thoughts which immediately grab the attention of his listeners.

> Last year, British manufacturing
> productivity rose by no less than 6 per
> cent—the biggest single jump in more
> than a decade. How was it done?
>
> To answer that question we have only
> to look at the changed climate of the
> UK labour market. We have made a
> decisive shift from the conflicts of the
> late Seventies to a new situation
> where flexibility and co-operation
> prevail.

He is off and away.

Troubleshooting

The chairman must be ready for emergencies.

The worst that can happen is for the speaker not to turn up on time—or at all. The unexplained absence can occur for all sorts of reasons: a sudden illness, a traffic jam, a double booking in an overcrowded schedule. Whatever the cause, if, after a decent waiting period (half an hour to an hour depending on the tolerance of the audience and the importance of the speaker) there is still no sign of the honoured guest (or any message from him), it falls to the chairman to make apologies and offer what he can by way of compensation.

> I am sorry, ladies and gentlemen, but
> I don't think we can wait any longer for
> Mr Tomkins. I have asked for refresh-
> ments to be served immediately. So, if
> you wouldn't mind moving to the back
> of the hall ...

Or

> I feel we should move to the second
> item on the agenda.

Or

> In the absence of Mr Tomkins, I
> suggest we proceed with a general

> discussion. I know there are a number
> of you burning to put questions or
> arguments. Can we start with you,
> Mr Jones?

This is not the time to show impatience or to get angry.

> Well, as you can see for yourself, our
> guest for the evening has not seen fit
> to put in an appearance. You might
> think he could spare the time to send a
> message but there we are, there's no
> accounting for manners...

It is at about this point that the speaker appears at the back
of the room, booming apologies for his late appearance. The
embarrassed chairman must then embark on the near-impos-
sible task of restoring the audience to a receptive mood.

If there are signs of anger at being kept waiting, the chairman might try to lift the spirits of the audience with a show
of good humour. But in these circumstances there is only
one joke known to have turned wrath into laughter. It was
made by the chairman of a political meeting in Dublin when
it was clear that the candidate had mixed dates and would
not, after all, be addressing this assembly.

> It is usual on these occasions for the
> chairman to say that the speaker
> needs no introduction. Well, this time
> it's literally true because the bugger
> hasn't turned up.

Somehow, it comes over best with an Irish accent.

There are occasions when the chairman can fill the gap left
by an absentee speaker — either by reading from a prepared
text which he has had the good fortune or good sense to
obtain in advance or by delivering his own views on the
subject under discussion.

The second option is a hostage to fortune in that the chairman will almost certainly not come up to the audience's
expectations. He is not the person they came to hear, he is
unlikely to know as much about the subject as the absentee
speaker and, since he has not done his homework, the standard of presentation will leave a lot to be desired.

When a speaker gives notice that he cannot fulfil his appointment, he may send a replacement. This is a common ruse for senior politicians who couch their acceptances of speaking dates with warnings that affairs of state must take priority. However excusable, there is an inevitable sense of let-down when in place of the great man there appears an unknown junior minister or parliamentary private secretary.

The wise chairman does not give away too much too soon. If, for example, a minister is due to put in an appearance in mid-conference, the chairman should not begin the proceedings with the news that the star turn will be missing from the programme. This would be to invite a mood of disenchantment and to make life difficult for the speakers who must come before.

Unless the rumours start flying ('Have you heard? The Minister has resigned!') it is best to hold off the announcement until the last moment.

The stranger on the platform will indicate to the audience that something is up. Now it is for the chairman to persuade the meeting that he is introducing someone worth listening to.

Lightly does it!

There is a story about that great actor, Sir Ralph Richardson, who, as you may know, was a little absent-minded. Walking to the theatre one evening he caught sight of someone he thought he knew. He boomed out a greeting: 'Well, if it isn't George Simpson. My goodness, George, you look well. You've lost weight, I can see. There's colour in your cheeks. And what about that moustache? I never thought I'd see you with a moustache!' The man interrupted: 'But I'm not George Simpson.' Richardson was unabashed. 'So, changed your name *too*, have you?'

Fortunately, I have not carried misunderstanding quite so far, though I must admit that when I met our guest in the lobby a short time ago it

was on the tip of my tongue to tell
him, 'You don't look a bit like Sir
James Frinton.' Well, as I need hardly
tell you, this is not Sir James, who
sends his apologies for his unavoidable
absence. But Sir James has done more
than send apologies. He has asked
Mark Henderson, Minister for
Overseas Investment, to come in his
place.

We are grateful to you, Sir, for
stepping in at such short notice. Your
reputation goes before you as a
politician of radical and forceful views.
We are eager to hear what you have to
tell us.

For the conscientious chairman there is only one prospect
more appalling than having to face an audience without a
speaker and that is having to face a speaker without an
audience. It is, of course, dispiriting to look out on rows of
empty seats but some speakers interpret a light attendance
as a personal insult. Unless reassured they are liable to work
off their displeasure on the few loyalists who *have* taken the
trouble to be present. Once again, it is the chairman who
must intercede with a few comforting words.

Circumstances are against us, I fear.
We have been hit by illness—the flu
bug is on the march again—and I have
had various apologies from those who
were unable to escape from prior
business commitments.

The end justifies embellishment of the facts (two apologies
might reasonably count as several) but not an outrageous lie.
A claim to know of dozens who have unavoidably missed out
on this thrilling occasion might impel the speaker to ask for
their names so that he can send them a copy of his address.
   The chairman should ensure that a small gathering is at
least a cosy one.

Would those of you at the back mind
moving forward to the two front rows?

A scattered audience is always difficult to handle and, anyway, looks smaller than the same number of people in a tight group.

Control

Once the speaker is up and away on his flight of rhetoric, it is tempting for the chairman to relax, to slide into a comfortable position in his chair, to let his thoughts wander to affairs beyond the meeting room. But this is to fail in his responsibility. If he is grossly inattentive, the audience will notice and take their lead from him. 'This man must be a bore; even the chairman can't stay awake.'

More seriously, the lazy chairman is ill prepared for any hitch in the proceedings — an attempt to interrupt by an obstreperous questioner, say, or a tendency by the speaker to run way over his allotted time.

Over-running is a frequent problem which calls for firm but tactful control. The seriousness of the offence depends on circumstances: ten minutes on top of an hour-long formal lecture is of no great consequence. But five minutes added to a 20-minute speech when other speakers are waiting their turn can start a chain reaction leading to the total disruption of a carefully planned schedule.

At some of the bigger conferences, a light on the rostrum flashes menacingly at any speaker who outstays his welcome. But generally it is for the chairman to exercise his authority in whatever way he feels appropriate. A written note slipped across to the speaker should do the trick but it does need to be clearly written — in bold capitals, preferably. A scribbled message which takes close reading to interpret will either be ignored or will confuse the speaker, making it even harder for him to finish what he has to say.

An instruction from the chairman should allow the speaker time for manoeuvre. 'TIME UP — STOP NOW' is as unfair as it is impolite. A more sensible message might read 'We are running short of time, please wind up.'

If this fails, the chairman has a right to interrupt. But he must choose his moment. The object is not to humiliate the speaker, which is the inevitable result of cutting him off in mid-sentence. The trick is to jump in at a point where the speech might reasonably conclude. Since long-winded speakers are addicted to the 'one last thought' syndrome it is not hard to spot the approach of a likely finishing mark. Such as:

> Above all, I want to emphasise the urgency of a decision. We cannot afford to wait.

Now!

> Thank you, Mr Jones. I must stop you there.

Mr Jones will undoubtedly suffer a moment of shock. He has at least six other vital arguments he wants to repeat by way of summary and he is not used to being interrupted. But it takes a very hard case indeed to resist a plain invitation to resume his seat.

And so to question time.

After the speech

If the audience is unduly passive it may be up to the chairman to start the ball rolling.

> I have a question that was handed to me earlier. Perhaps we can start with that.

Or

> While our audience is gathering its thoughts, I have a question of my own I would like to ask.

More questions will soon follow. And not only questions. At least one member of the audience will want to embark on a speech of his own.

> Will the speaker please tell us where we are to find the money for such an ambitious scheme? I know from my own experience how difficult it is to persuade the powers that be to allocate sufficient resources to...

Away he goes, carried along on a succession of thoughts

which can only serve to distract attention from the main event. The chairman must intervene. This is easy enough to do because with a questioner he does not have to worry about the propriety of interrupting a train of argument.

> I feel we're in danger of losing track of the question. Now, if I understand you correctly, what you want to know is...

Vote of thanks

The chairman's duties end with a proposal for a vote of thanks to the speaker.

He may use the opportunity to summarise the proceedings, pointing up what he sees as the salient arguments. This leads into some words of praise for the speaker. Even a mediocre performer deserves credit for making the effort.

> On behalf of everyone here I would like to thank you for taking the time to speak to us. You have given us much to think about.

A really good speaker is entitled to something more. But a string of superlatives can sound forced, and, anyway, is likely to make the audience cringe.

If the words of appreciation are to make their intended impact, they need filling out in some way. A light-hearted anecdote can do the trick.

> George Bernard Shaw used to tell of a man whose ability to utter streams of profanity held all listeners spellbound. The day came when this monumental blasphemer was moving house. On the steep hill outside his former home, the tail-gate of the removal van gave way and everything he owned in the world went crashing down into the street. The neighbours gathered in tense expectation of an outburst of cursing that would put all previous effort in the shade. But our hero only shook his head. 'I cannot do justice to the occasion,' he sighed.

Now, of course, it is not my intention to swear and curse at our guest. On the contrary. I have nothing but praise for him. But in listening to his speech and thinking about my concluding remarks, I wonder if I can do justice to the situation.

Let me put on record simply that this has been among the most enjoyable and interesting of our events. Thank you, Mr Jones, for giving us such a splendid address and for leading such an exhilarating discussion. I know I speak for everyone when I express the hope that you can be persuaded to return before long.

No more need be said. The hackneyed invitation to the audience to 'show their appreciation in the usual way' only serves to demean the vote of thanks. If the chairman wants applause all he has to do is to lead the way. When he joins his hands together, the audience will follow suit; and in showing his enthusiasm he will swell the volume of approval from the body of the hall.

9

Chairing the In-House Meeting

Chairing a meeting from a platform with an audience out in front is, for most of us, an occasional duty. Chairing a meeting of business colleagues gathered round a conference table is an everyday occurrence.

A senior manager can spend up to 70 per cent of his time in meetings—seeking or imparting information, collecting opinions and deciding on strategy. His skill as a chairman may well represent the difference between the success and failure of his department or company.

Is the meeting justified?

A chairman who knows his job takes time for a periodic re-assessment of the value of each meeting. Does it produce results? If not, why not?

A meeting can fail because:

It has outlived its usefulness
When two or three come together for a specific purpose, it is often quite difficult to break them of the habit even when their purpose has been achieved.

> Thank you, gentlemen. That just about wraps it up. But I suggest we meet again to assess developments. Some time next month?

And the month after that, and the month after that...

The wrong people are invited

It may seem good politics to ask Tom and Harry to put in an appearance, even though they are not directly involved in the matters to be discussed. After all, they hate to feel left out.

But however sensitive Tom and Harry may be, it cannot serve their interests or those of the meeting to have them sitting in as spectators. Either they will get bored, transmitting their mood to others, or they will feel the need to throw in extraneous comments which can only serve to distract from the subject in hand.

The meeting is held in the wrong place

The conference room may be too small (with everyone crowded together and feeling thoroughly disgruntled) or too large—which can inhibit discussion.

In an efficiently managed meeting each individual needs a comfortable upright chair (an easy chair is an inducement to slumber), a flat surface for a spread of papers and a clear view of everyone else in the room. It is near impossible to argue a point effectively if at the same time you have to crane your neck to see whoever it is you are trying to persuade.

The object of the meeting is unclear

There is rarely any difficulty in finding something to talk about. Whether the conversation is relevant to the meeting is another matter. The only way of making sure that everybody talks to the point is to have a written agenda—and to stick to it.

It is up to the chairman to create the conditions in which his meeting will have the best chance of success.

He must be clear in his mind that:

- The meeting has a useful purpose.
- The right people attend.
- The meeting is held in appropriate circumstances at a mutually convenient time.
- An agenda is circulated well before the meeting.

Thereafter, what actually happens at the meeting depends on what the chairman (assumed to be the senior manager present) wants out of it.

In theory, a meeting is justified on the principle that two or three or more brains are better than one. As a result of an open and rational assessment of the issues, a consensus view emerges which is then enshrined in the form of executive policy.

Reality, however, is less in tune with the democratic ideal.

Typically, a meeting is held to reinforce a decision already made by the chairman of the meeting or a manager senior to him. Changes in details may be acceptable but in broad terms nothing said at the meeting can alter the direction of policy.

Why then hold the meeting? To provide information, probably. But also to win the active support of managers for the new policy and, through them, the support of the entire workforce.

Advocacy

The chairman must see himself in the role of advocate. It is not enough for him to make a bold announcement.

> Right then. I've called you together today to tell you that the new factory is not to be built at Sunnyfields after all.
>
> Instead, the whole shooting match is to go to Greyacres. I know this will come as a surprise to some of you, but there it is. It's up to us to make sure the new plan is a success. Any questions?

There are managers who take this to be the forthright manner of a born leader. In fact, it is playing at dictator — and intelligent employees resent the implication of servitude. To gain their co-operation, the chairman needs to give reasons for the policy change and to leave time to answer objections.

> We had no choice but to withdraw from Sunnyfields when it became clear that we could not achieve a single-union agreement. You will remember that we stipulated a single union deal

> as a precondition of such an ambitious investment.

The production manager is bursting to say something. Wisely, the chairman defers to him.

> But why Greyacres? The area has a long history of bad labour relations. And unless I'm much mistaken, the general level of education and training is not up to the standard we need.

No doubt others at the meeting feel the same way. The chairman must be ready to answer their criticisms.

> The worry about training was voiced by several directors when the proposal was first put to the board. But after visiting Greyacres I'm much more confident. Conditions have changed a lot in the last few years. Of course, there's still a lot to be done in the way of providing adequate training. That's where you come in, Jim. We'll need all your expertise to prepare a first-class training programme.

This chairman knows what he is about. Assuming the responsibility to explain policy, he deflects opposition with an appeal for constructive co-operation. The chairman and business leader are as one.

Keeping people in touch

A second type of meeting has to do with maintaining contacts between people in the same or similar occupations. The weekly or monthly sales meeting is an example familiar to most businesses. Sales people, especially those who spend much of their time on the road, can easily get cut off from mainstream company affairs. They welcome the opportunity to meet together with their colleagues to hear about product development and promotion initiatives and to compare sales performances.

The secret here is to put all contentious issues at the head of the agenda. If the meeting is in part justified by the need for people to let off steam, it is far better that they should have their say early on. To leave the problems to the end is to risk closing the meeting on a sour note—if, indeed, it is possible to close the meeting at all. A fit of the grumbles, with the force of suppressed energy behind it, can take an age to work itself out.

Moreover, if someone with an ache to voice an opinion has to sit through an entire agenda before being given his chance to speak he will ignore all other matters except that foremost in his own mind.

By the same token, the best news should be left until last. In the sales meeting it might be the announcement of some outstanding figures or of a product breakthrough which can transform the market. The aim should be to send everybody away with the enthusiasm and determination to keep up the good work—or to do even better.

Consensus-seeking

The third type of meeting is the one that is run on more or less democratic principles. Here, the chairman is in the role of interviewer, seeking out information and opinions in the hope of reaching a consensus.

One can imagine this happening when, for example, a board elects a new director. This is not the moment for a full-scale debate on the candidate's qualities—presumably there has been some consideration of his suitability prior to the critical meeting. But the outcome may still be in doubt.

> Next on the agenda is the vacancy for marketing director. Of a shortlist of three, Bob Mitchell of Alpha Martin has emerged as the clear favourite. But before going any further I do want to give everyone here a chance to express an opinion.

This is the chairman's way of saying that there may be reservations about Bob Mitchell. He wants to bring their worries out into the open. The first to speak is Henry Temple, one of the old guard, a senior member of the company who feels that marketing is a much overrated profession.

> There is one point I would like to
> raise. I know that Mitchell has made a
> great success of Alpha Martin but it
> doesn't follow that he will make a
> great success here. We are an entirely
> different company in an entirely
> different industry.

The argument deserves consideration. It is not enough to shout down the critic. The chairman needs unanimous support for such a vital appointment. After all, the marketing director will be working closely with all other departmental heads. To start at loggerheads with one of them could be disastrous.

The chairman decides to try balancing the argument by introducing another point of view.

> What do you say, Norman? You've led
> the way in beefing up the marketing
> department. Do you think Bob
> Mitchell's experience is relevant?

> Yes I do. I feel very strongly that the
> principles of good marketing apply to
> all companies whatever they happen
> to produce.

This comment gives the chairman the opportunity to open up the discussion.

> Would anyone else like to give an
> opinion?

There follows a short general debate with the chairman making sure that no individual, either for or against Bob Mitchell, is allowed to dominate.

Noting that one director remains silent, the chairman makes a point of encouraging him to have his say.

> What about you, Robert? We haven't
> heard from you yet.

Robert is bound to respond.

> I had my doubts about Mitchell. But
> after this meeting I'm inclined to
> think that we should take the plunge.

> Certainly we need a stronger
> marketing thrust. If anyone can do it,
> it must be Bob Mitchell.

This positive view, expressed by someone who has done more listening than talking, is an opportunity for the chairman to draw the discussion to a close. Opinion is running in favour of Bob Mitchell. No doubt Henry will remain sceptical but, if properly handled, he will accept the majority view.

> Given the timetable we have set
> ourselves, we must have a decision on
> this matter. It is clear that the
> meeting favours making an offer to
> Bob Mitchell. But this is not to
> dismiss Henry's reservations. There
> are features of our company which
> make it quite different from Alpha
> Martin. Bob Mitchell will need our
> help and support in adjusting to a new
> commercial environment.
>
> To explore how this might be done, I
> suggest an early meeting between Bob
> Mitchell and Henry. Does that suit
> you, Henry?

Almost certainly, the idea *will* appeal to Henry. Outvoted (but without the humiliation of a formal vote) his pride is satisfied in a way that will allow his ready acceptance of the board's decision.

For this, as for all other meetings, the responsibilities of the chairman continue beyond the adjournment. While there may be a secretary on hand to take the minutes it is up to the chairman to ensure that a fair record of the proceedings is circulated without delay. Those nominated by the meeting to implement decisions must know precisely what they have to do and by when.

A good set of minutes can serve as the framework for the agenda of any follow-up meeting. If the minutes do not specify action of any sort, it is a fair assumption that a further meeting is not required.

10

The School Visitor

It used to be the custom for head teachers to ensure an enthusiastic reception for a speech-day guest by allowing him to announce a half-holiday. Nowadays, this concession is a rarity (teachers jealously guard all easy claims to popularity) which means that a visiting speaker from the world outside the school gates must work harder to keep the attention of his audience.

Young people en masse are notoriously difficult to please. Talking down to them is to invite derision; talking up will produce blank incomprehension. The same might be said of any audience, of course, but the chances of failing to hit the right level are greater with youngsters simply because most adults are not used to handling them in groups.

A good start is not to hand out gratuitous advice. It is in the very nature of young people to believe that, at the very least, their elders are none too bright. They will do something only if they think there is a good reason for doing it, and a hand-me-down platitude of experience does not count as a good reason.

Opening with a pithy quotation on this very theme can help to establish friendly relations.

> 'I have found that the best way to give advice to your children is to find out what they want and then advise them to do it.'
>
> *Harry S Truman*

Or, from the point of view of the younger generation:

'I have lived more than 30 years on this planet and I have yet to hear the first syllable of valuable or even earnest advice from my elders.'

H D Thoreau

Instead of urging this or that particular way of life, the speaker should concentrate on opening up possibilities, offering choices, stimulating ambition. It is up to you, he is saying; all I can do is to point out the directions.

The warning about not getting too specific in doling out advice applies with equal force when the discussion turns to earning a living.

For example, the head of an engineering company is invited to speak at his local comprehensive school. His first inclination is to detail the life of the skilled technologist, with reference to his own experience and to his success in creating a thriving business. But then he gives some thought to his audience. What might be appropriate for the sixth-form science group is set in too narrow a context for an audience of mixed interests and ages.

There is more mileage, he decides, in looking at business as a whole and in talking about the opportunities for making a worthwhile career in industry.

You will be taking up your careers at a period when there will be greater opportunities than ever before.

I know that at the moment there are worries about unemployment. Young people are finding it difficult to get any sort of job, let alone the jobs they really want. But this might change. Because of the smaller size of families nowadays we can expect a 30 per cent drop in the number of school leavers by the early 1990s. Youth unemployment will be a thing of the past.

But increasing demand for bright young people will not remove the need to get the best possible qualifications — and experience. Employers vary considerably in their capacity, and willingness, to provide opportunities for training and career advancement. So shop around — check out those employers who are keen to develop staff potential by encouraging further education.

Many business careers cross the boundaries of academic disciplines and thus appeal to a wide audience. One such is sales and marketing.

I have just read some encouraging news. Among jobs highly favoured by young graduates, sales and marketing figure in the top five. I have never known this happen before. A decade ago, sales and marketing would barely have scraped into the top 20 — and then only for those who had taken less than brilliant degrees.

Why the change?

For the answer, you only have to look at the new breed of business leader. Unlike their predecessors who were brought up to believe that market forces were essentially stable and predictable, the latest generation of tycoons have won their spurs in an intensely competitive economy.

This, in turn, is the product of the technological revolution.

In business after business, the force of advanced technology has simplified the manufacturing process. Old established companies are no longer able to rely on experience and tradition to hold off competition. Given the financial resources, entrepreneurs with bright ideas can break into markets hitherto dominated by the aging giants.

But it is one thing to invade a market — quite another achieving staying power.

> To succeed, a product must sell. And
> to win sales, against rivals at home
> and abroad who are just as capable of
> turning out quality products, a
> business needs top salesmen. The
> rewards and status of salesmanship
> have risen accordingly.

The message that the rewards go to those who work hard
enough—irrespective of academic standing—always goes
down well. Here again, a relevant quotation gives force to
the argument:

> 'There is no such thing as a great
> talent without great will power.'
>
> *Balzac*
>
> 'There is no such thing as a great man
> or a great woman.
>
> 'People believe in them, just as they
> used to believe in unicorns and
> dragons. The greatest man or woman
> is 99 per cent just like yourself.'
>
> *G B Shaw*
>
> 'The average man is always waiting
> for something to happen to him
> instead of getting to work to make it
> happen. For one person who dreams of
> making fifty thousand pounds, a
> hundred people dream of being left
> fifty thousand pounds.'
>
> *A A Milne*
>
> 'You can do anything in this world,
> if you are prepared to take the
> consequences.'
>
> *W Somerset Maugham*

Scoring a laugh with a young audience is a most difficult
thing to do. (Unless by accident—an unintentional pun, say.)
  It is a fair guess that the set-piece jokes—the source of all
conversations beginning 'Have you heard the one about...?'

are already well known. In fact, most of these stories seem to enter popular currency via the school grapevine.

But personal reminiscences can be fun, particularly if they relate to classroom misdemeanours.

Cracks about education are permissible if they originate with someone else. To cite a well known personality—one who has thrived in life after school—is to draw the sting from the most outrageous comments.

> 'There is nothing on earth intended for innocent people as horrible as school. It is in some respects more cruel than a prison. In a prison, for example, you are not forced to read books written by the warders and the governor.'
>
> *G B Shaw*
>
> 'One of the ultimate advantages of an education is simply coming to the end of it.'
>
> *B F Skinner*

But the richest source of humour is the mores and manners of earlier generations.

Pick at random an old volume of *Boys' Own* or *Girls' Own Paper* (available at all good second-hand bookshops). The Victorian earnestness of these journals gives a joyous insight into the worries that used to beset young people.

> 'Folly wishes to know,' wrote the Editor of the *Girls' Own Paper* agony column, 'whether, if the harness of her carriage were put in order by a gentleman who happened to be passing, meeting him afterwards she should "move towards him."'' The advice was unequivocal. 'Do not on any account do that. It might be alarming should he have sensitive nerves. A slight bow in passing would be quite sufficient.'
>
> And of another girl: 'As to her receiving letters from a man with whom she is not even acquainted, it is

utterly disgraceful, not to say
undutiful. The man who would dare to
compromise a girl in such a way,
unknown to her parents, deserves the
horsewhip!'

While the incredulous expressions are still fixed, the speaker
can lead in to his finale.

So you think you've got problems!

11

Happy Birthdays

Birthday speeches are chiefly for the middle-aged and elderly. Young people at parties are impatient with speakers—
rightly so. It takes a skilled performer to compete with the
latest rock group. But the 21st birthday party is an exception. At this celebration it is still customary for an elder
(usually the one who is footing the bill) to say a few words.

> Thank you all for coming. As the
> spokesman for the older generation, it
> falls to me to propose a toast to youth,
> and to one young person in particular.

A personal note might come in here showing how the speaker
connects with the birthday boy or girl.

> Looked at from my vantage point and
> remembering—just—what it is like to
> be young, I can see that there are
> several advantages in being 21.
>
> It is an age when parents can be seen
> at their best. Having surrendered all
> authority—assuming they ever had
> any—they are now available, on call,
> as hoteliers (full board, minimum
> rates), chauffeurs (late night parties a
> speciality) and bankers (loans repaid
> over long periods at nil interest).
>
> Twenty-one is an age when all adults
> of advanced years—those over
> 30—can be seen in their true light.

Past their best and getting a bit soft in the head.

More seriously

By the same token, those of or above the magic age are, to use Dr Johnson's phrase 'towering in their confidence'.

It is time for being up and about, for grabbing opportunities, for doing great things.

To Peter, I say:

Make the best of it. Of all that I can see of the energy and talent of this generation, you have a good chance of realising your hopes.

An example of Peter's achievements so far might be inserted here.

Anyway, I wish Peter every good fortune. And I ask all his friends to join with me in drinking to his health and happiness.

Birthday celebrations for the middle-aged can be a way of easing the pain of knowing that another year has vanished into thin air; for the elderly it is more a recognition of achievement, an annual victory over fate at ever-lengthening odds.

Either way, the birthday party speaker should keep cheerful and look to the future. Advanced age should not be allowed to rule out a sense of pleasurable anticipation.

It is often said that as we get older we take life more gently. The age of maturity is also the age of sober reflection.

How dull! I refuse to believe it!

The second half of life can be more exciting, more fulfilling than anything that has gone before. To prove this, I have all the evidence I need here at this party. In celebrating the birthday of Lilian Green, we are celebrating a milestone in a life packed with activity. Never once have I known Lilian to turn away from a challenge — even when the pressure of other responsibilities was at its greatest.

And so it will go on. For next year, Lilian's diary is already pretty full.

If any of you hope to fix up a meeting with Lilian before her next birthday, I suggest you check out a few dates right now.

Lilian, you are an example to all of us — thank you for being you and for adding so much to our pleasure of living. On behalf of everyone here, I wish you a very happy birthday — and many more birthdays to come.

To lighten the mood still further, here are a few all-purpose birthday quotations.

'The only thing that bothers me about getting older is that when I see a pretty girl now it arouses my memory instead of my hope.'

Milton Berle

'The years between 50 and 70 are the hardest. You are always being asked to do things, and you are not yet decrepit enough to turn them down.'

T S Elliot

'Growing old is more like a bad habit which a busy man has no time to form.'

André Maurois

'Being 82 is getting up in the middle of the night as often as Burt Reynolds, but not for the same reason.'

Bob Hope

'Age has its compensations. It is less apt to be brow-beaten by discretion.'

Charlie Chaplin

Interviewed on his 77th birthday, Harold Lloyd told an interviewer: 'I am just turning 40 and taking my time about it!'

'Every man over 40 is a scoundrel.'

G B Shaw

'To me, old age is always 15 years older than I am.'

Bernard Baruch (American financier)

Asked if, at 90, he still chased girls, George Burns replied, 'Only down hill.'

'I have a bone to pick with fate
   Come here and tell me girlie,
   Do you think my mind is maturing
                                late,
   Or simply rotted early?'

Ogden Nash

Responding to congratulations on reaching his century Adolph Zukor, founder of Paramount Pictures, commented: 'If I'd known how old I was going to be, I'd have taken better care of myself.'

12

Toasting the Bride and Groom

After the menopause, the critical change in life is when the invitations to speak at weddings are outnumbered by the invitations to speak at memorial services.

There are those who keep to roughly the same speech for both types of event—'known A for many years, fine upstanding person, count our blessings, look to the future' etc—the all-purpose bland expressions of amity related to times past. While this approach is acceptable for a memorial, the wedding should be a celebration of the future at which certain reminiscences—'I remember the days when she stood just so high'—can be mawkishly inappropriate.

As an old friend of one of the families central to the occasion, the speaker at a wedding party will not be short of material. But he has to take care not to upstage the bride and groom, their parents and sundry relations who may be wondering why they have not been invited to address the assembly.

Consequently, it is best not to get too personal (another reason for steering clear of the reminiscences) and instead look more to the institution of marriage and to what it holds for these young people.

A framework begins to take shape.

- What do we know about marriage?
- It is a much maligned and battered social custom.
- Despite this, more people are getting married than ever before. For most of us, it is better than the alternatives.
- There can be no general formula for a successful marriage.

- This is why advice from the older generation is seldom of much value.
- But every couple has within them the resources to make a success of marriage.

From the speech-maker's point of view, the virtue of marriage is that it has inspired a great many quotable observations, for and against.

'It looks as if the Hollywood brides keep the bouquets and throw away the grooms.'

'The husband who wants a happy marriage should learn to keep his mouth shut and his check-book open.'

Groucho Marx

'My recipe for happiness in marriage? Good health and a bad memory.'

Ingrid Bergman

'Husbands are like fires. They go out when unattended.'

Zsa Zsa Gabor

'The concept of two people living together for 25 years without having a cross word suggests a lack of spirit only to be admired in a sheep.'

A P Herbert

'I've had friends who when they marry say, "I know we're going to have to work at it." I always think they're wrong. The things that are really pleasurable in life, whether it's playing softball or working on your stamp collection, really require no effort.'

Woody Allen

'Would I consider remarriage? If I found a man who had fifteen million dollars, would sign over half of it to

me before the marriage and guarantee
he'd be dead within a year.'

Bette Davis

'They say marriages are made in
Heaven. So are thunder and
lightning.'

Clint Eastwood

'I'm a firm believer in getting married
early in the morning. That way if it
doesn't work out you haven't wasted a
whole day.'

Micky Rooney

'I would love to get married again,
provided two conditions are met: that
I am in love and that I am backed by
the Ford Foundation.'

Gig Young

'I want a man who only has to be kind
and understanding. Is that too much
to ask of a multi-millionaire?'

Zsa Zsa Gabor

'I spent so much on my wife, I decided
to marry her for my money.'

Richard Pryor

Such riches must be used sparingly. A speech loses its individual character if it is overloaded with quotations. One or
two will be quite sufficient.

Ladies and gentlemen.

You don't need me to tell you why
we're here. You might need me to tell
you *how* we came here...

(A reference to the inevitable problems some guests had in
finding their way from the church to the reception.)

And, after this excellent champagne,
you may need someone—but not me—
to tell you how to find your way home.

But setting aside these minor complications, this must count as one of the great days of our year. The celebration of the marriage of Tom and Sophie is an event which gives us all enormous pleasure. Such an attractive and talented couple can, I am sure, look forward to a bright and exciting future.

Said with a smile　But we must not underestimate the risks and hazards of the step they are undertaking.

The married state has come in for a lot of battering in recent years. The cynics are a powerful force, even if few would go so far as Micky Rooney. He claims that he always gets married in the morning; then, if it doesn't work out, he hasn't wasted a whole day.

Ah, well, there will always be those for whom marriage does not measure up to expectations.

I prefer to take a more optimistic view and with Tom and Sophie I believe I have good cause for optimism. The quality I detect in them which will ensure their happiness is generosity, based on sympathy and understanding.

I have a selfish reason for being delighted that this is so.

It removes any need for me, or anyone else, to offer worthy advice. Tom and Sophie are quite sensible enough to handle their own lives without the pearls of wisdom from the older generation.

But I would leave them with one thought—not so much a piece of advice as an observation based on experience.

> In this confusing world, we all have a
> need for someone on whom we can
> depend, for better or worse.
>
> The value of marriage is not that it
> turns two people into a couple, but
> that it can help a couple grow as two
> individuals. With all the pain and
> difficulty that entails.
>
> No matter what the prevailing
> morality, marriage has always been
> the greatest risk we can take and the
> bestower of the deepest potential
> happiness. Of course, every marriage
> is something of a gamble. But unless
> you gamble, you can't win.

The celebration of the second or third marriage for either the
bride or groom calls for an even greater determination to
look forward. This most certainly is not the moment for
speculation on what Tom or Mabel might think if they were
around to see this. References to earlier partners, now de-
ceased or discarded, are fraught with risks of acute embarrassment.

> When was it? Can it really be five
> years ago when George was taken
> from us? After that tragic accident on
> the bobsleigh run, I well remember
> thinking to myself that Grace could
> never find another such noble partner
> to accompany her through life. How
> wrong I was. For I detect in Bill, as I
> once detected in George, all the
> qualities which mark him out as an
> exceptional person.

On the face of it, these remarks, if a little over the top, are
not offensive. But the speaker is making some bold and
potentially dangerous assumptions. One can only hope that
Bill does not resent comparison with George. However, the
chances are that in the first flush of love he is a little sensitive on the subject of his predecessor. As for Grace, her
memories of the fine sportsman who was her dear husband

may now be tarnished by the realisation that he spent more time on the ski slopes than with her. All in all, it probably is wisest to leave George out of it.

> The omens are good. This is a marriage of matching personalities; of like minds. Individually, Grace and Bill have many of the talents that go to make a successful and happy life. Together they are unbeatable.

The best opening for a speech celebrating the marriage of an older couple was delivered by Sir Harold Wilson at the wedding of the nonagenarian Emanuel Shinwell. He denied rumours that the bride's father had forced the couple into a shotgun marriage.

13

Retirement

Retirement is a touchy subject for conversation—and for speech-making.

For all those who look forward to an extended holiday on a comfortable income, a greater number anticipate the end of a working life with severe apprehension. It means starting all over again, finding things to do at an age when the possibilities may seem tightly confined.

The problem takes on mammoth proportions when the workplace is the pivot for all social as well as professional activities. The soon-to-be-pensioned-off employee—often one who is loyal and dedicated to a fault—imagines that he is losing his very reason for being. A presentation clock and a few words of good cheer from his senior manager are not likely to make the prospects more inviting.

At its most extreme, the problem of coming to terms with retirement will not be solved by a farewell speech, however skilfully composed. But forethought and consideration can produce a speech best suited to the occasion and—in the case of an employee who may have to be dragged kicking and screaming from the premises—one that is at least calculated not to exacerbate his emotional crisis.

To start with a common example of where things can go badly wrong, consider the case of Bill Simmons, a middle manager of some 25 years' standing, who, at the age of 56, is facing the prospect of early retirement.

It is clear that Bill does not want to go. It is equally clear that to send him off with words of praise for his unique contribution to the company may serve only to fuel his resentment.

149

If he is so valuable, why are they letting him go? At the same time, it would be gratuitously offensive to quote Bill's years of sterling service.

The way out of the quandary is to follow the rule for imparting bad news. Be positive!

> We will miss Bill. But our loss is a mighty gain for the Rural Conservation League. Bill is founder member of our local RCL branch and one of its most active supporters. The RCL will, I know, benefit enormously from the extra time Bill can now give to this excellent cause.

Nine times out of ten the departing employee has a hobby or leisure activity the speaker can catch on to. A little research may be necessary to establish the facts but there is no need to prove an unqualified commitment. If, say, it is not immediately apparent that Bill intends to throw himself heart and soul into the Rural Conservation League, the speaker can be excused for anticipating events.

> As we all know, the RCL is dear to Bill's heart. I very much hope that from now on he will be able to devote more of his time and his organisational talents to the work of the League.
>
> It needs more supporters like Bill if it is to fulfil its ambitious programme.

The idea may not have occurred to Bill but the speech might set him thinking—'Yes, there is something I can do.'

Early retirement should be seen as part of a natural progression in business life, not as a sign of failure. Emphasise the contribution Bill, or whoever, has made to bringing on the younger generation, those who are now beginning to take over the reins.

> We owe Bill our gratitude for his expert supervision of the computerisation programme. Some of the best of our junior managers have Bill to thank for the quality of their training.

Having taken the sting out of the occasion, it is then permissible to recall the highlights of a career—but without overstretching the story. In the heady atmosphere of a retirement party it is easy to embark on a long and, for its listeners, a wearisome trip down memory lane.

> I well remember the time when CB—(most of you won't remember CB; he was general manager from '56-'65, a great character). Anyway, as I was saying, I well remember...

You can almost feel the weight on the eyelids.

But there is nothing against a straightforward account of Bill Simpson's progression up the company ladder.

> Bill came to us in 1954, a trainee in the accounts division. He was quickly spotted by the finance director as a manager in the making and as early as 1960 he was in charge of his own department.

At this point a dip into the files can revive a few memories.

> I have found a comment on Bill's performance after one year's service. It says here that he was conscientious, industrious and a stickler for time.

The next part is open to poetic licence.

> Well, he hasn't changed very much, I'm glad to say, though I remember a succession of late morning arrivals. On the fourth occasion, as luck would have it, Bill came through the doors at precisely the same moment as the then chairman, Sir Percival Grimwade. 'Late again, Simpson,' observed the chairman nastily. 'Yes, Sir Percival, I'm afraid you are,' replied Bill before disappearing into his office.

A life in business is bound to throw up a few funny stories. But make sure they are not already well known to the audience. Also, there are some stories that are best forgotten.

What happened at the notorious New Year's party of 1967 probably fails on both counts.

End on a note of good cheer.

> We wish you and your family every happiness. This is not a goodbye because there will be many occasions when old friends meet up. It is then that we will bore you with talk of office politics while envying you your sun-tan.

It would be handy to end on a quotation but for a retirement speech the choice is restricted. Comments on the subject by famous men tend towards cynicism. Ernest Hemingway said it all when he decided that retirement is 'the ugliest word in the language.'

But R C Sheriff has left us with a neat observation on the traditional retirement gift.

> When a man retires and time is no longer a matter of urgent importance, his colleagues generally present him with a clock.

14

In Memoriam

The memorial service is intended to be the antidote to the funeral, transposing a sense of loss with loving memories. Its success depends on treading a thin line between thanks for what has been and regrets for what might have been.

The speaker at a memorial service can usually be counted upon to know his subject. A close friend or colleague of, let us say, the lamented James Stilton, one-time celebrated business man and community leader, will have no trouble in delving back for suitable material. James was a good family man, dedicated to making a success of his company while pursuing a variety of interests. Recollections of his campaign to attract overseas investment to an area of high unemployment will be warmly received and there has to be a mention of his close involvement in numerous charitable enterprises.

The difficult part is to assess James's character in a way that his family and friends will appreciate. As with most of us, his virtues are not unequivocal. Those who praise his bluff, no-nonsense manner are offset by critics of his rough handling of certain delicate issues. Moreover, a strongly expressed regard for social responsibility did not prevent him from closing one of his factories when times were hard.

But a memorial service is not the time for objective analysis. Without necessarily quoting the controversial features of a life story, the aim must be to put the best possible interpretation on events.

What are the strongest memories of James as a person?

He was a loyal and generous friend.

He was an inspired businessman who had the knack of keeping one step ahead of the game.

By example, he persuaded other employers to provide more jobs for the disabled.

He held firm opinions and was not afraid of stating his own views. (The other side of the coin was his stubbornness, and inability to compromise.)

He had a great sense of fun.

Listing the characteristics which mark out someone as an individual is a powerful memory-jogger. Stories come to mind which help to fill out the portrait of the man. The speech begins to take shape.

We are here to pay tribute to an extraordinary man.

In the last few days I have frequently asked myself if it is at all possible to describe the hugely varied life of James Stilton in just a few words. And I came up with a phrase which I think personifies James in all his achievements. The phrase is self-made.

The mood is established—serious but in no way depressing. The listeners are intrigued because 'self-made' is not a description they would automatically apply to James Stilton. In the memorial address as much as in any other speech, the aim is to catch the interest of the audience early on.

Now, I am not suggesting that James came from a desperately poor or deprived family. He had a comfortable upbringing; he was bright and he was ambitious.

But he was also a great one for spotting opportunities and grabbing at them. It is in that sense that he could claim to be self-made.

Now is the moment to engage the enduring memories.

> I remember when we were both young men setting out on our careers, it was James who was determined to be his own boss. I am ashamed to say, I never gave him very much encouragement. To me, his schemes were wildly unrealistic.

> It was all very well talking about setting up on his own. But where was the money to come from? Where would he find the premises?

> Well, as we all know, James raised a loan—not much, but enough—and he set up his first business in an old cinema, a real flea pit where for years the audiences had been numbered in single figures.

> The owner couldn't believe his ears when James put in a bid for the place. He was even more amazed when James told him that he was planning to turn the building into a factory to make men's clothing.

> The last film they showed at the old Central starred Alec Guinness. It was called *The Man in the White Suit*. Very appropriate.

The joke is appropriately mild and should be delivered likewise. The speaker is inviting smiles, not loud laughter.

> As we all know, James went from strength to strength. He had a wonderful talent for anticipating the customer. He could tell you what clothes you would be wearing next year, even before the designers had got up from their drawing boards. And he was usually right.

It is about time we heard something of the family. Wife and children and other close relatives are central to the occasion and need to be drawn into the speech at the first opportunity.

> I said earlier that James was self-made. Now I must backtrack somewhat on that opinion because, of course, he would not have got anywhere without the love and support of his wife Ann, and their children Mark and Julie.
>
> It was a united family; a family that lived life to the full.
>
> Mark and Julie are grown up now and have families of their own but I have not forgotten the days when they were very young, playing on the tennis court James made for them—and always beating their father. James was keen on sport but was not himself the best of players. The only time he beat me at golf, I had my leg in plaster.

Another soft joke with the punchline almost thrown away. The point will not be missed.

Now we come to the difficult part. Some mention must be made of the controversial element in the career of James Stilton. But criticism of the way he ran his affairs, justified no doubt, should be seen in perspective.

> James was tough-minded; he had to be. He took many difficult decisions which, inevitably, were the cause of much controversy. But whether for or against James Stilton, all those who had dealings with him agreed on one point. He was always fair—and straight.
>
> He was never afraid of saying what he believed. And having said it—he was a man of his word.

This leads to a high point in the life of James Stilton, his public service and work for charity. We have all that is needed for a fitting climax.

Many of us have reason to be grateful to James's acts of great kindness. I don't think he ever turned away anyone who came to him asking for help.

His unstinting efforts on behalf of our community will long be remembered. Many of us thought he was hopelessly optimistic when he started his campaign to bring new money—and employment—to this town. Thankfully, he proved us wrong. Our present prosperity is in no small measure the achievement of James Stilton.

But there was another great cause, even dearer to his heart. His sympathy for the disadvantaged made him a powerful spokesman on behalf of the disabled. James made us aware of our unconscious prejudices against those who do not fit the norm. Once, when we were in a lift together, he got very angry about the way the control panel was designed. I didn't know what he was on about until he made me imagine what it was like to sit in a wheelchair and have to try to reach the button for the top floor.

It was by example that he proved to other employers the all-round benefits of creating more jobs for the disabled.

There could be a reference here to individuals who have supported James in his work or who have particular reason to be grateful to him.

I began by saying that James Stilton was an extraordinary man.

Perhaps it is only now that he has gone that we realise just how exceptional he was.

He will be missed by family and friends. But he will not be forgotten.

15

Receiving and Giving Awards

A speech of acceptance at an award ceremony is one of the most difficult acts to put across convincingly.

For a start, there is the strong temptation for the speaker to assume too much. Not one of us is immune to the flattery of public recognition, however big or small the occasion.

The adulation afforded to stars of stage, screen and high finance at their annual back-slapping ceremonies has its small town equivalent in the awards handed out for services to the company or the community. At both ends of the scale the risk is the same: that the recipient will actually come to believe destiny has marked them out as extra special. That's when vanity takes over.

As the much-praised actor Herbert Beerbohm Tree observed, 'The only man who wasn't spoiled by being lionised was Daniel.'

> Ever since I was a small boy I have dreamed of this moment. I remember as well the day my father took me to one side and said, 'You know, son, you have great talents; don't waste them. And then and there I made a pledge to dedicate myself to the benefit of my fellow man.

It doesn't take much more of this to start stomachs churning.

As bad, if not worse, is the prizewinner who goes to the other extreme with a surfeit of false modesty.

> In accepting this wonderful award I
> want you all to know how much I owe
> to dear Betty who, when times were
> hard, was always there to give a
> helping hand. With Betty I must
> couple the names of George and Fred,
> whose dedication and hard work have
> made it all possible. And last but not
> least, to Mum and Dad, I would say
> just this...

The feeling of distaste at this demonstration of inverted
pride must not be allowed to overwhelm a basic truth—that
few awards are achieved by a single-handed effort. Some
recognition of the wider contribution does not go amiss.

With this in mind, let us try for a gracious, not arrogant,
acceptance speech which makes proper acknowledgements
without declining into sycophancy.

> You do me a great honour. It would be
> foolish to deny that over the years I
> have wondered a few times how I
> might react to such an occasion as
> this. Like us all I have had my
> ambitions and like us all I have
> dreamed of achievement. You might
> call it an excess of hope over
> expectation.

> But today, for me, fantasy becomes
> reality. And, I must tell you, my
> reactions are not as I anticipated. I
> always expected an overwhelming
> sense of pride. I've arrived! Success!
> I've done it!

> But it's not like that. Oh yes—I'm
> proud to be here, proud also that I
> have been selected for this great
> compliment. But far stronger than
> pride is the sure knowledge of how
> much I owe to my colleagues. When
> young, this possibility never occurred
> to me. If I was going to make it, I would
> do it on my own. Now, I am wiser. I
> know that without the unfailing help

and support of good friends, my efforts would have led nowhere.

Therefore, ladies and gentlemen, in accepting this award, let me say thank you—to all of you—for making it possible.

Accepting an award on behalf of a company or other organisation calls for a shift of emphasis and of tone.

In speaking for Beaumont Brothers as I am often called upon to do, I have to face up to the difficulty of blending the opinions of my colleagues.

Said tongue in cheek   Contrary to popular opinion they are not always in total agreement. But heaven help me if I ever appear to misrepresent the company view.

On this occasion, however, I have no such worries. I know, as a matter of certainty, that everyone at Beaumont is proud and delighted to share in this magnificent award.

On behalf of all my colleagues, I thank you.

Handing out awards is much easier than accepting them. Often, a simple announcement will do.

And the winner of this year's Community Service Medal is (long pause) Andrew Cooper. (Loud cheers.)

When a more fulsome introduction is needed, the standard rule applies—be brief, be relevant.

This year's Festival of the Arts would not have been possible without Andrew's singleminded devotion to the project. That we have enjoyed such wide recognition for our efforts is entirely due to Andrew's inspired leadership.

By way of response, Andrew will put in a modest disclaimer

but will be delighted by the recognition of his part in the success of the festival.

On a more general level, every business has its incentive awards—from a Caribbean holiday for the top salesman to an engraved plaque signifying ten years' service on the staff consultative committee.

Such awards can come in a rush, at an end-of-year party, say, or at a sales conference. At these mass presentations the first consideration is to get the details right. All incentive goes out of the window if the chairman muddles the names or job-titles.

> Now what do we have here? Ah, yes, a bottle of champagne for... Now, who is it exactly? I can't read my own writing... Oh, I see, it's for Bill Huggett. What's that you say? Jill Huggett? Oh, it's for Mrs Huggett. Now how could I have forgotten Mrs Huggett?

But he did. What is more, that same Mrs Huggett, hitherto a loyal member of staff, now thinks that the chairman is an idiot.

A presentation must be counted as special; otherwise it is not a presentation.

> Jill Huggett has been with us for ten years, five of them as chief telephonist. Unfailingly kind and helpful, she has achieved as much for business as anyone on the staff.

A sincere compliment, graciously delivered. Duly flattered, Jill Huggett will return to her post determined to do an even better job. As a way of motivating staff, the presentation speech is simple and effective.

16

Appearing on Television

Television interviews are for masochists. The experience can be punishing but the afterglow is exquisite.

The very thought of all those millions—well, thousands—of viewers hanging on every word, boggles the mind and inflates the ego. No wonder it is rare for anyone to turn down the opportunity to appear on screen.

That said, it is surprising how few interviewees prepare themselves for the great event. A little thought on how best to put across an argument in the unfamiliar and unreal circumstances of a broadcast interview can do wonders for a performance.

Case study: Reacting to adverse publicity

Consider the ordeal of Frank Knightsbridge, chairman of Dee Construction, a building firm which specialises in quality homes for middle-income families. With the steep rise in housing prices, Dee Construction has made a point of minimising costs by pioneering building techniques which save on labour and materials. For several years the company has enjoyed flattering publicity while the reputation of Frank Knightsbridge as a go-ahead entrepreneur has grown apace.

But now there is a risk of public confidence evaporating. There are reports that some Dee Construction customers are complaining of shoddy workmanship in their new homes.

One paper decides to make an issue of what is headlined the 'scandal of the jerry builders'. The first Frank Knightsbridge knows of it is when he opens a copy of the *Daily Shout*, to see a double-page attack on his company with pictures of outraged home buyers pointing to cracked walls and sagging roofs.

Having barely recovered from this shock he takes a call from a reporter on a rival paper who has been told by his editor to follow the story up. Understandably angry and upset, Frank relieves his feelings with a stream of invective against muckraking journalists, ending up with a threat to sue the *Daily Shout* and any other paper which dares to malign the good name of Dee Construction.

This is a serious mistake, as Frank soon realises. He should have held the reporter off until he had checked the facts. He could have done this quite simply by promising to ring back after investigating the story. By responding without first considering the case for the defence, he has merely helped fuel the rumours of serious malpractice.

All this comes out in Frank's subsequent meeting with his public relations consultants. By now, it is clear that the problems are limited to one housing estate in the country town of Netherington, where pre-fabricated building units have proved to be faulty. The decision is taken for Dee Construction to accept full responsibility for the error and to carry out immediate repairs. Morally correct, the policy of reparation also makes sound business sense. Dee Construction is set to recover its valued reputation for fair dealing.

The question is, how best to stage the counter-attack against the *Daily Shout*? The PR advice is to try for a television current affairs programme with a high audience rating called *Watchdog*. If the editor can be persuaded to accept Frank as an interviewee, this will be his best chance of responding quickly and forcefully to the adverse publicity.

But the PR people are worried about Frank's capacity to handle a full-blooded television interview. To minimise the risk of their plan backfiring they propose a television training session in which Frank can try his communication skills in front of the camera. Having made one blunder in his dealing with the media and not wishing to fail a second time, Frank readily agrees to the idea.

This is what he learns:

Get to know the interviewer
If possible, have a preliminary chat about the format of the programme and general tenor of the questions.

Do not expect to be told in advance the precise nature of every question. If the interviewer is any good he will adopt a flexible approach, adapting his line of questioning to take advantage of unexpected twists in the conversation. But even if he is the unimaginative type who has planned a strict sequence of questions, it is best for the interviewee not to know. Otherwise, he will start mentally rehearsing his replies which he will then deliver with all the passion of a speak-your-weight machine.

Assume that the interviewer is friendly
Contrary to popular opinion, the typical interviewer is not beset by an urge to humiliate his guests. Even if raised in the aggressive school of interviewing he knows that an audience is quick to react against questioning which is unduly harsh or otherwise unfair.

In any case, in the time available (usually three or four minutes) more genuine information is likely to be gained from a softly-softly interrogation in which the interviewee feels confident enough to express himself openly.

Be comfortable
Given the tension created by any formal interview it is impossible to be entirely relaxed. But this does not mean that the interviewee must tolerate an uncomfortable chair or be inhibited from asking for a glass of water.

Start strongly
Viewers are blessed with the privilege of switching channels or switching off if they do not happen to like what is on the screen. To hold attention, an interview must establish its interest in the first few seconds. This is especially true if the first question is pathetically tedious ('Tell me, Mr Knightsbridge, what does it *feel* like to be called "the bungler of the building trade"?'). The interviewee needs to respond forcefully and persuasively.

'Is that what they're calling me? Well, I think the charge is entirely unjustified and I'll tell you why...'

At the sound of an authoritative voice belonging to someone who is evidently not afraid of stating his opinions, the viewers begin to sit up and take notice.

Listen to the questions
A common fault is for the interviewee to answer the question he would like to have heard instead of the one that is actually put to him.

> INTERVIEWER: Mr Knightsbridge, these are serious complaints. What do you intend doing about them?
>
> FRANK: My company has an excellent record in giving value for money.

Maybe so, but that is not an adequate or even a very sensible reply.

Speak clearly and to the point
There is an urge to use long words and involved phrases — 'an impressively outstanding achievement' for 'a job well done', for example. Or 'remunerative employment' for 'work'.

This tendency to elaborate is an instinctive device for marking time, giving the interviewee the chance to think through what he really wants to say. But the advantage, if it exists at all, is very slight and is more than outweighed by the risk of boring an audience with unnecessary and sometimes incomprehensible verbiage.

Avoid abbreviations and acronyms
To viewers who are not in the know a reference, say, to the BF will raise images unassociated with the Builders Federation.

Beware statistics
A few relevant figures can add weight to an argument but a bevy of statistics can sink it.

Watch out for clichés
Someone once defined a cliché as the simplest way of making a statement. The hackneyed phrase is a natural part of

ordinary conversation—we cannot hope to be original all of
the time—but relentless repetition is a turn-off. Among the
abused clichés currently in fashion, 'at the end of the day'
and 'at this moment in time' are probably the most irritating.

Do not try to take over the interview
This trick is favoured by politicians, who feel that brow-
beating an interviewer somehow confirms their qualities of
leadership. But the one who dominates—be it interviewer or
interviewee—by talking too much, quickly loses the sympathy of the audience.

Never be afraid of saying 'I don't know'
Few questions are so complex as to draw a blank response,
but anyone can be caught out by an occasional stinger.
Waffling does not help—the interviewer is merely encouraged to repeat the question or to ask an equally knotty
follow-up—and guessing is dangerous. There is always
someone who delights in putting the record straight while at
the same time making the interviewee look foolish or, at
worst, dishonest. It is far better to accept defeat gracefully:
'I'm sorry but I simply don't know the answer.'
    It is a response which gains marks for candour and com-
pels a welcome switch in the line of questioning.

Watch out for the trick question at the end
A live interview is timed to the last few seconds. When the
moment comes for the interviewer to round off the discussion, he may do so by delivering a question which requires a
short, snappy answer.

> Do I take it then that you have no
> intention of resigning?
>
> No.
>
> Thank you.

This final question can be the most difficult for the interviewee because it puts him on the spot. But he must answer
strongly. To prevaricate is to leave on a note of anticlimax
which can wipe out any good impressions created earlier in
the interview.

To summarise:

Be brief—be clear—be relevant.

Having worked his way through the basic principles of interviewing, Frank Knightsbridge is ready for a dummy run. His television trainer sets the scene. Frank is to be quizzed for three minutes in a face-to-face studio interview. This will follow a filmed report on the grievances of house buyers in Netherington.

The session begins with a studio introduction to the story.

> When is a dream house more like a nightmare? 'When the ceiling falls in', says Mrs Thompson of Netherington in Suffolk. It happened just three weeks after she moved into her new home. And she is not alone in her complaints. Her neighbours too are having their problems, as Jane Burnett discovered.

The film is a succession of diatribes against Dee Construction, one estate resident after another showing off the defects in their houses. 'What can be done', asks the reporter, 'to help these people? Their answer is clear enough. Knock down the houses and start again. The question is will Dee Construction agree?'

As the film ends, the presenter turns to Frank Knightsbridge.

On the right of the page is a verbatim report of their discussion. On the left side are the comments of the public relations adviser who is monitoring the transmission.

> INTERVIEWER: With me is Frank Knightsbridge, chairman of Dee Construction. Well, Mr Knightsbridge, what about it? Are you planning to start again at Netherington?
>
> FRANK: I don't think the position is that serious.

Oh dear. He sounds
very defensive. Why
didn't he start on a
more positive note?

INTERVIEWER: Judging by the film
it looks bad enough to me.

You asked for that
one.

FRANK: No doubt. But, if I may say
so, your film is very one-sided. Dee
Construction is not a fly-by-night
company. We have thousands of
satisfied house buyers.

Still too defensive.
Anyway, the
presenter is not
suggesting that the
entire company is
rotten. Get to the
point.

INTERVIEWER: I'm not sure I understand. Are you saying that because
most of your customers are happy, the
minority who do have complaints are
not worth worrying about?

Advantage again to
the interviewer; and
he's not even trying.
Frank must do some-
thing to pull the
argument his way.

FRANK: No, of course I'm not saying
that. All our customers are held in
equal esteem.

A bit pompous.

FRANK: I am merely trying to make
the point that we are not the sort of
company to walk away from problems.
We will do our level best to rectify
matters at Netherington.

Better. But why
qualify the offer of
help? 'Our level
best' may not be
good enough.

INTERVIEWER: And how do you
propose to do this?

FRANK: Well, we've already started
the ball rolling with a full investiga-
tion into the causes of the complaints.

By now, the typical
viewer will think he
is trying to avoid
the issue. And time
is running out.

INTERVIEWER: I should have thought
the causes are obvious enough— cracked
walls, ceilings falling in...

FRANK: Yes, quite. But we need to
know why these things are happening.
Is there a structural fault, for example,
or are we dealing with substandard
building materials which, for reasons
we have yet to ascertain, fail to meet the
requisite standards of the BSA?

What on earth is the
man talking about?

INTERVIEWER: The BSA?

FRANK: The Building Standards
Authority.

INTERVIEWER: I see. But surely
this is a side issue. Whatever the
reasons for the poor state of these
houses, the fact is the residents are
suffering *now*. What can you do to
help them?

The interviewer is
beginning to lose
patience; and who
can blame him?

FRANK: Repairs will be carried out as soon as possible.

INTERVIEWER: Can't you be more precise?

FRANK: Not at this moment in time.

Terrible prevarication.

INTERVIEWER: Are you talking about days or weeks or months?

FRANK: Oh, not more than two or three weeks, I should think.

Why couldn't you have said that at the start?

INTERVIEWER: So, within a month at most, Mrs Thompson and her neighbours will be happy people again.

FRANK: I sincerely hope so.

You don't sound too confident.

INTERVIEWER: One last question, Mr Knightsbridge. Are you intending to pay compensation for the inconvenience these people have suffered?

FRANK: Well, that is a matter we are still considering. We want to be fair but it is not so easy to arrive at a decision when there are so many factors to take into consideration and er...

Pure waffle.

INTERVIEWER: In a word, Mr Knightsbridge. Is compensation likely or not?

FRANK: Er, yes. I think so.

INTERVIEWER: Thank you.

Ah well. Back to the drawing board.

That was a bad interview stopping not far short of catastrophe. What went wrong?

A quick reading of the transcription may suggest that the interviewer was tough and uncompromising. But his questions were really quite straightforward. He was simply not prepared to be fobbed off with vague answers.

It was Frank Knightsbridge who was at fault.

By starting weakly he lost the initiative; he wandered from the point; he was long-winded and failed every time to give a straight answer to a straight question.

The training session continues as word comes through that *Watchdog* does want Frank to appear. An hour later a car arrives to take him to the studio. He is soon on his way to his second screen interview of the day. Only this time it's for real.

> INTERVIEWER: With me is Frank Knightsbridge, chairman of Dee Construction. Well, Mr Knightsbridge, what about it? Are you planning to start again at Netherington?
>
> FRANK: Only in the sense that we won't make the same mistakes twice. I believe we can repair the damage quite quickly.
>
> INTERVIEWER: Don't you think you might have trouble in persuading the Netherington residents of your good intentions? We have just heard some pretty serious accusations of neglect by your company.
>
> FRANK: I don't want to minimise the seriousness of the complaints but even if the cause of the problem is a structural fault, which is the worst that can happen, the renovation should not take too long.
>
> INTERVIEWER: How long?
>
> FRANK: Four weeks at most. We have already started work and, I might add, we would have started earlier if the residents had come directly to me instead of to the press.

INTERVIEWER: You say there may be a structural fault. Shouldn't you have known about this before you started building?

FRANK: A structural fault is a possibility, nothing more. If it does exist, yes, of course we should have known. But like everyone else, we make mistakes occasionally. And we correct them.

INTERVIEWER: Does that mean you'll be paying compensation?

FRANK: We will make amends for any inconvenience we may have caused.

INTERVIEWER: Can you put a figure on it?

FRANK: No, for the simple reason that every case must be judged on its merits. But I want all our customers to feel that we treat them fairly and squarely. On that principle I am not prepared to compromise.

INTERVIEWER: Mr Knightsbridge, thank you.

That was so much better. Frank Knightsbridge gave every impression of knowing what he was talking about. By responding clearly and directly to questions, he inspired confidence. In both interviews the facts of the case were precisely the same. But the contrast in the way those facts were presented made all the difference between scepticism and credibility.

It is the same with all forms of public speaking. Even the best argument can fail for want of presentation.

In the words of the song: 'It's not what you say: it's the way that you say it!'

17

Radio Interviews

All the rules of TV interviewing apply to radio—and then some.

The trouble with radio is that it is deceptively easy. A reporter with a tape recorder turns up at your home or office and invites you to talk. There is no compulsion to hold back; you can say what you like for as long as you like. Tape is cheap and there is plenty of it.

But the freedom to range widely in recorded conversation has its penalties. The more you say, the more that will have to be edited out for transmission. And the more that is edited out, the greater the risk of falling victim to editorial interpretation.

Some interviews end up as a succession of comments taken out of context. But the interviewee has no redress.

Good radio demands self-discipline. Find out how much time the interviewer wants to fill—and then try to stick to that limit.

If, as often happens, the interviewer wants to talk about several topics or several aspects of the same topic, it can make sense to divide the recording session into self-contained sections. This way there is less risk of confusing the issue by veering back and forth between the main arguments.

Hold on to the fact that there is only one way of commanding the attention of a radio audience. The voice is all. An otherwise dull TV speaker might attract viewers by his natty suiting or extravagant gestures. (The audience may not be listening too closely but they will at least be looking.) On radio, there is no fallback. Listeners are utterly ruthless.

With a flick of the switch, a tedious or irritating voice will be despatched to oblivion.

To heighten interest in whatever you have to say, vary the pace of delivery; the monotone is a great inducement to slumber.

Resist the pursuit of red herrings. The interviewer may not be deliberately leading you astray, merely exploring possible lines of interest. But if you feel the conversation is irrelevant, you are not compelled to go on with it.

Keeping in mind these and other rules discussed under the heading of television interviewing, we can listen in on an interview with a businessman who finds himself making news—though not the sort that is generally welcomed.

Defensive interviewing

The questioning opens on an assertive note.

> INTERVIEWER: After five years of spectacular growth your company is suddenly under pressure. How do you account for this change of fortune?

The question cannot be avoided. It calls for a constructive and, as near as practicable, an optimistic response.

> BUSINESSMAN: You seem to be suggesting that we're facing a crisis. This is simply not true. This year's results are disappointing, I'm the first to admit, but they're made to look worse than they really are because people expect us to come out on top.

The interviewer is not so easily diverted.

> INTERVIEWER: But until recently you were full of confidence. What went wrong?

It is time for a little more detail.

> BUSINESSMAN: The sharp and unexpected increase in interest rates came at a bad time for us. We had just embarked on an ambitious programme

of investment in new technology. This
cost us a lot more than we anticipated.
At the same time, some of our more
important overseas customers
trimmed back on their orders. We
were hit both ways at once.

INTERVIEWER: Do you see an early
recovery?

It is easy to go over the top on such a deceptively easy question.

BUSINESSMAN: Oh yes!
Everything is fine now. We'll be back
on form in a month or two.

But this is to invite a sharp follow-up.

INTERVIEWER: Well, you got it
wrong before. What makes you think
you have the answer this time?

The truth is, he is not really sure that he does have the
answer. The inclination is to flannel in the hope that no one
will notice the reluctance to give a direct reply. But they will.
Let us try again.

INTERVIEWER: Do you see an early
recovery?

BUSINESSMAN: I am sure we'll see
a recovery. Whether it is early or not
is another matter. The company is in a
strong position. We are not afraid of
competition. But there are factors
beyond our control. Earlier I
mentioned high interest rates. I hope
we will see the cost of borrowing come
down very soon. But that is for the
government to decide, not me.

This is a more realistic—and convincing—response. But it is
not necessarily strong enough to divert the interviewer.

INTERVIEWER: Are you saying
that if interest rates remain high there
will be no recovery?

> BUSINESSMAN: No, I am not saying recovery depends entirely on a fall in interest rates. But if the cost of borrowing remains high we will have to consider a change of strategy. We are never short of problems but I have yet to come across a problem which cannot be solved.

The reply effectively closes the discussion on matters which, in any case, are largely speculative. Rashly expressed opinions on what may or may not happen some way ahead can become a useful source of ammunition for competitors and critics.

But the interview still has a little way to go.

> INTERVIEWER: Talking of problems, are you worried by the rumours of a possible takeover of your company?

A subtle question. A straight answer—Yes—may fuel unwelcome speculation. But No is patently a lie. Who would not be worried by rumours of a takeover?

> BUSINESSMAN: There are two ways in which I can answer you. The first is to say that if the company is attractive to buyers, I take it as a form of flattery. We must have something that they—whoever they are—think is worth buying.
>
> The second point is this. To be successful a takeover must have the support of at least one of the major shareholders. At the moment, there is no indication at all that any of them are prepared to sell.

It may be that a more direct answer is called for.

> BUSINESSMAN: I assume you are referring to the 6 per cent interest acquired by AOB Holdings. I am sure they have made a wise investment but

> my board would strenuously oppose a
> full-scale takeover. We do not see how
> the company will benefit by
> absorption into a giant conglomerate.

There may be follow-up questions but when at this stage of
an interview an opinion is expressed firmly — and, by implication, finally — the interviewer is inclined to take his chance
to wind up the discussion.

> INTERVIEWER: John Barton.
> Thank you.
>
> Cut.

Different types of radio interview

Studio and down the line

If an interviewee is invited to a studio for a one-to-one session, he should not necessarily expect the interviewer to be
there to welcome him. Their discussion may very well be
conducted 'down the line'. The interviewee sits alone in a
small studio (usually about the size of a broom cupboard)
while his questioner talks with him from another studio in
another town or even another country.

It is sometimes argued that the impersonal nature of a
down-the-line session leads towards a forced and awkward
style of interview. But the experience is no different from
the telephone conversation which all businessmen take in
their stride.

No doubt, the main reason for dissatisfaction springs
from the interviewee's expectations. Unless he is very
experienced in dealing with the media, he makes his way to
the studio anticipating the full treatment, with a comfortable studio, a flesh-and-blood interviewer and a line up of
technicians ready to spring into action when (inevitably)
something goes wrong with the machinery. But nowadays
this rarely happens. The expansion of radio output (think of
the profusion of local radio stations) has been achieved by
cutting costs to the bone. Along with everyone else in radio,
interviewees are expected to rough it.

Chat show and phone-in

The one-to-one interview used to dominate in radio current affairs. But no longer. We are in the age of the chat show and the phone-in.

The risk of the chat show is saying too much or too little. Where there are several participants in a free-for-all discussion there will be one dominant personality. The producer must make sure of this to protect himself against the conversation drying up—a prospect not to be countenanced by a programme-maker who wants to hold his job.

The star guest is readily identifiable. His name and reputation mark him out as the one who is to have the last word—and quite a few other words as well.

But he should know that an abuse of his privileged position can easily antagonise an audience. A speaker who will not give anyone else a chance to contribute will be dismissed as an arrogant know-all—and rightly so.

Equally, the guest lower down the pecking order who allows himself to be bullied into silence will lose respect. There is no love lost on the browbeaten.

Listeners do respond to a speaker who states his views convincingly; who refuses to be shouted down, yet listens politely to those willing to abide by the normal rules of conversation; and who responds constructively to opposing arguments.

Assume the topic of conversation to be the rejuvenation of the inner cities.

The guest at the head of the pecking order is a rumbustious politician who can be relied upon for contentious opinions. Among the other participants is a businessman whose company has an inner-city base.

The politician launches into the debate in typical aggressive style.

> POLITICIAN: In my view there is no virtue in the government throwing good money after bad. Money alone will not solve the problem of the inner cities. What is needed is the will to succeed and this can only come from the people themselves.

This glib opener annoys the businessman who knows only

too well that 'money' and 'will to succeed' cannot be isolated in separate compartments. But he knows enough not to fly off the handle.

> BUSINESSMAN: The distinction is unfair. Self-respect depends on getting respect from others—including the government. There is not much hope for the inner cities unless more money is spent on improving the infrastructure.

The response is predictable.

> POLITICIAN: Nonsense! Give me just one instance of government funding of inner-city projects where the money has not been misused or wasted.

This is a familiar trick question used by politicians to put their opponents on the defensive. The natural reaction is to try desperately to think of a suitable example. The chances of success are slim. Whatever is suggested will be thrown back at the proposer.

> POLITICIAN: Call that an example of good investment? If that's the best you can come up with, you've proved my case.

To avoid the trap our businessman simply refuses to go into detail at this early stage of the discussion.

> BUSINESSMAN: There'll be time enough to talk about specific examples. Don't you think we ought to settle on some basic principles first of all?

Then he turns the questioning so that the other speaker has absolutely no chance of avoiding a direct reply.

> BUSINESSMAN: Are you saying that you would refuse all government funding to the inner cities?

Now the politician is on the defensive.

> POLITICIAN: No, of course not.
> What is important is to make sure
> that the taxpayers' money is not
> thrown down the drain.

It is the moment for a conciliatory gesture.

> BUSINESSMAN: I quite agree with
> you. As a businessman who has
> practical experience of the inner cities,
> I find that the chief problem is trying
> to deal with too many government
> agencies. We need less talking and
> more action.

It is at this point that the chairman decides to put in a word.
It might well be asked why he has not intervened before.
But the chairman is not there to put his point of view. He will
only break in if he feels that the conversation is running out
of steam or if, as now, he spots an interesting line of enquiry
which he thinks should be followed up.

> CHAIRMAN: You say you want more
> action. What exactly do you have in
> mind?

Here is a golden opportunity for the businessman to win
over his audience. For half a minute or more (a long time on
air) the speaker has the microphone to himself. To make best
use of his time he must put across his arguments clearly and
succinctly.

> BUSINESSMAN: If the people of the
> inner cities are to give of their best,
> they must have somewhere decent to
> live. For the most part, housing
> standards are appalling. Rebuilding
> and renovation should be top
> priorities.
>
> The second priority is to work for
> higher standards of education—for all
> age groups. I want to see a general
> rise in the level of expectations. At the
> moment, nobody expects very much

> because the mood in the schools and colleges is essentially pessimistic. I want them to start teaching the truth—which is that anything is possible if you put your mind to it.

The politician can hardly disagree with this last sentiment.

> POLITICIAN: I thoroughly endorse what you say about the need for higher aspirations. The question is how can this be done without gross over-spending? Now, one idea I would like to put forward is this...

And so the discussion moves into top gear with an assessment of likely innovations. Thanks to the skilful contribution of the business representative, what could so quickly have become a slanging match has developed into a constructive but lively debate. Listeners will at least remember the programme—which is more than can be said of so much current affairs output.

It is easy to understand why the phone-in is so popular with the broadcasting planners. As the only really successful application of community radio, the direct involvement of listeners in debating current affairs can be achieved at modest expense since the contributors come free of charge.

To be at the centre of a phone-in—the studio guest who fields the questions—can be an invigorating experience. Over half an hour or so one can talk to an enormous range of people who express a wide, sometimes wild, variety of views.

The skill of the guest speaker is in adapting to the tone and style of each of the questioners. Few of them have more than a vague idea of what they want to ask before they come on the air. They are liable to get to the point by a circuitous route and may go on indefinitely unless politely but firmly interrupted.

> CHAIRMAN: It's your question Mr Jones.

> CALLER: Thank you. Good morning Mr Wilkins. Now, you're a successful businessman. You have factories all over the country and all over the

> world, I shouldn't wonder. Now, what
> I want to ask is this. Why is it, with
> all these factories, why is it you're not
> taking on more workers? I mean we've
> got thousands on the dole, it's just not
> right...

The caller is well away on what is clearly an emotive theme.
It is vital to break in on his ramblings—but in a way that
does not offend or patronise.

> CHAIRMAN: You've raised a very
> important point, Mr Jones.

Nobody minds being interrupted to be paid a compliment.

> BUSINESSMAN: This is a big
> question.

It certainly is. The speaker has the problem of framing an
answer without resorting to vague generalisations. It would
be so easy to proclaim the enterprise economy—the impressive growth in national income, the trend towards higher
levels of employment which must, at some unspecified
future date, embrace all those who are willing and able to
work. Easy—and meaningless.
   Instead, he fastens on to a particular aspect of the question, one that may not even have occurred to the questioner.

> BUSINESSMAN: It is true that my
> company employs a large number of
> people, and would employ more if we
> had the chance. But the sad fact is
> that those who need work are not
> necessarily qualified for our highly
> technical industry. Now, this mis-
> match seems to me to be critical to the
> future of the entire economy. Over the
> whole country the jobs will go to those
> who can adapt to advanced
> technology. The opportunities for
> training and retraining are to hand. It
> is just a case of persuading more
> people to take advantage of those
> opportunities.

A general question has drawn a specific response—which is the way it should be. The chairman moves on to the next call.

> CHAIRMAN: We have a question about the cost of packaging. Are you there, Mrs Tadworth?

> CALLER: Yes. And I'd like to know why companies like yours, Mr Wilkins, spend so much on fancy packets and boxes. I have one of your products here and I'm told that half the cost of its production goes in packaging and promotion. I think that's disgraceful. The customer is not made of money, you know.

The caller is plainly put out by what she sees as an unfair imposition. It would be fruitless to antagonise her further by an outright denial of her claims. There is more sense in trying to bring down the level of antagonism to a point where a rational exchange of views is possible. This can be done quite easily by starting on a note of accord.

> BUSINESSMAN: I agree with you Mrs Tadworth. Too much *is* spent on packaging and promotion.

You can almost hear the wind escaping from the sails.

> BUSINESSMAN: But the fact is, the typical customer prefers to buy products which are attractively packaged. We know this because when there is a choice between simply packaged low-price goods and fancy packaged higher-priced goods, we always sell many more of the latter. I realise it may not be of much comfort to you, Mrs Tadworth, but if we followed your wishes on this matter, we would soon go out of business.

Next question.

The phone-in holds its audience as long as it maintains pace. Those who ring in with questions and opinions are invariably unpractised speakers who have trouble organising their thoughts. It is up to those in the studio to keep up the momentum.

Further Reading from Kogan Page

The Business Guide to Effective Speaking, Jacqueline Dunckel and Elizabeth Parnham

Effective Meeting Skills: How to Make Meetings More Productive, Marion E Haynes

Effective Presentation Skills, Steve Mandel

How to Communicate Effectively, Bert Decker

How to Make Meetings Work, Malcolm Peel

Improving Your Presentation Skills: A Complete Action Kit, Michael Stevens

Readymade Business Letters, Jim Dening

Readymade Interview Questions, Malcolm Peel

Speak with Confidence, Meribeth Bunch